The Invented State

JOURNALISM AND POLITICAL COMMUNICATION UNBOUND

Series editors: Daniel Kreiss, University of North Carolina at Chapel Hill, and Nikki Usher, University of San Diego

Journalism and Political Communication Unbound seeks to be a high-profile book series that reaches far beyond the academy to an interested public of policymakers, journalists, public intellectuals, and citizens eager to make sense of contemporary politics and media. "Unbound" in the series title has multiple meanings: It refers to the unbinding of borders between the fields of communication, political communication, and journalism, as well as related disciplines such as political science, sociology, and science and technology studies; it highlights the ways traditional frameworks for scholarship have disintegrated in the wake of changing digital technologies and new social, political, economic, and cultural dynamics; and it reflects the unbinding of media in a hybrid world of flows across mediums.

Other books in the series:

Journalism Research That Matters
Valérie Bélair-Gagnon and Nikki Usher

Voices for Transgender Equality: Making Change in the Networked Public Sphere
Thomas J Billard

Reckoning: Journalism's Limits and Possibilities
Candis Callison and Mary Lynn Young

News After Trump: Journalism's Crisis of Relevance in a Changed Media Culture
Matt Carlson, Sue Robinson, and Seth C. Lewis

Press Freedom and the (Crooked) Path Towards Democracy: Lessons from Journalists in East Africa
Meghan Sobel Cohen and Karen McIntyre Hopkinson

Data-Driven Campaigning and Political Parties: Five Advanced Democracies Compared
Katharine Dommett, Glenn Kefford, and Simon Kruschinski

Borderland: Decolonizing the Words of War
Chrisanthi Giotis

The Politics of Force: Media and the Construction of Police Brutality
Regina G. Lawrence

Authoritarian Journalism: Controlling the News in Post-Conflict Rwanda
Ruth Moon

Imagined Audiences: How Journalists Perceive and Pursue the Public
Jacob L. Nelson

Pop Culture, Politics, and the News: Entertainment Journalism in the Polarized Media Landscape
Joel Penney

The Invented State
Emily Thorson

Democracy Lives in Darkness: How and Why People Keep Their Politics a Secret
Emily Van Duyn

Building Theory in Political Communication: The Politics-Media-Politics Approach
Gadi Wolfsfeld, Tamir Sheafer, and Scott Althaus

The Invented State

Policy Misperceptions in the American Public

EMILY THORSON

OXFORD
UNIVERSITY PRESS

Oxford University Press is a department of the University of Oxford. It furthers
the University's objective of excellence in research, scholarship, and education
by publishing worldwide. Oxford is a registered trade mark of Oxford University
Press in the UK and certain other countries.

Published in the United States of America by Oxford University Press
198 Madison Avenue, New York, NY 10016, United States of America.

© Oxford University Press 2024

All rights reserved. No part of this publication may be reproduced, stored in
a retrieval system, or transmitted, in any form or by any means, without the
prior permission in writing of Oxford University Press, or as expressly permitted
by law, by license, or under terms agreed with the appropriate reproduction
rights organization. Inquiries concerning reproduction outside the scope of the
above should be sent to the Rights Department, Oxford University Press, at the
address above.

You must not circulate this work in any other form
and you must impose this same condition on any acquirer.

Library of Congress Cataloging-in-Publication Data
Names: Thorson, Emily, author.
Title: The invented state : policy misperceptions in the American public /
Emily Thorson.
Description: New York : Oxford University Press, 2024. |
Includes bibliographical references and index.
Identifiers: LCCN 2023033280 (print) | LCCN 2023033281 (ebook) |
ISBN 9780197512333 (paperback) | ISBN 9780197512326 (hardback) |
ISBN 9780197512357 (epub)
Subjects: LCSH: Political culture—United States. | Misinformation—United States. |
Polarization (Social sciences)—Political aspects—United States. |
Public opinion—United States. | United States—Politics and government—21st century. |
United States—Politics and government—Public opinion.
Classification: LCC JK1726 .T54 2024 (print) | LCC JK1726 (ebook) |
DDC 306.20973—dc23/eng/20230829
LC record available at https://lccn.loc.gov/2023033280
LC ebook record available at https://lccn.loc.gov/2023033281

DOI: 10.1093/oso/9780197512326.001.0001

Paperback printed by Marquis Book Printing, Canada
Hardback printed by Bridgeport National Bindery, Inc., United States of America

Contents

Acknowledgments   vii

1. Introduction: Misperceptions that matter   1
2. The contours of the invented state   14
3. The policy gap in the information environment   36
4. The construction of beliefs about policy   56
5. How people interpret policy information   75
6. Policy misperceptions and competence   98
7. Dismantling the invented state   116
8. Conclusion: What comes next?   133

Notes   145
References   149
Index   163

Acknowledgments

This book took a long time to write. And although the drawn-out process was not without frustrations (if only I could go back and re-run some experiments from half a decade ago!), it also made the book much better, largely because I was able to benefit from the advice and guidance of so many people along its meandering path to completion. In addition, the lengthy timeline has made it possible for me to integrate some of the amazing work that has been done in the past decade in the realm of misinformation and misperceptions. When I started working in this area, misinformation scholars were lucky to get a single conference panel. A decade later, misinformation was the theme of the 2023 American Political Science Association annual conference. I hope that this book contributes to a new direction for this field, as we collectively begin to (1) take more seriously the larger structural causes that lead people to hold false beliefs and (2) better identify the circumstances under which those false beliefs pose problems for democratic functioning.

The studies in this book were only possible because of generous funding from the Democracy Fund, the Knight Foundation, and the Campbell Institute of Public Affairs at Syracuse University.

While this book is not based on my dissertation, it still owes a huge debt to the incredible professors I worked with at the University of Pennsylvania. Diana Mutz's careful, practical approach to experimental design is without doubt the most important thing I learned in graduate school. I am also indebted to Dick Johnston, Joseph Cappella, Michael Delli Carpini, and Marc Meredith for all of their guidance both in graduate school and beyond.

The writing of this book spanned three jobs. I began the manuscript at George Washington University, and my first presentations of my interview data received fantastic feedback from Kim Gross, Dave Karpf, Matt Hindman, Steve Livingston, Will Youmans, Nikki Usher, and Caitie Bailard. Emily Kaplan helped with the initial interviews that formed the basis of the book. At Boston College, I am indebted to Dave Hopkins and Kay Schlozman for their feedback, and to Grace Denny and Adam Martin for assisting with the news content analysis.

In 2019, I held a book conference at Syracuse at which Jon Ladd and Jenn Jerit provided invaluable advice that improved the manuscript in a number of ways. Many of my colleagues also attended and gave helpful comments, including Chris Faricy, Margarita Estevez-Abe, Peggy Thompson, Dimitar Gueorguiev, Simon Weschle, Seth Jolly, and Brian Taylor. And an extra helping of thanks to Shana Gadarian, who not only took invaluable notes at the book conference but has also been a constant source of help and encouragement throughout my time at Syracuse. Finally, several Syracuse undergraduate and graduate students helped with the book's content analyses, including Nick D'Amico, Emma Dreher, Krisnina Magpantay, and Dylan McDonald.

Many other colleagues have also played a role in improving the book, either directly or indirectly. Thanks to Daniel Kreiss, Fabian Neuner, Chris Wlezien, Alex Coppock, Ethan Porter, Thomas Wood, Leticia Bode, and Emily Vraga for their insights, and in particular to Lisa Fazio and Briony Swire-Thompson for correcting my misreadings of the psychology literature. Thank you also to Adam Berinsky and the attendees of his 2019 MIT American Politics conference.

This book is delayed partly because of my involvement in the Facebook and Instagram 2020 Election Study, but the experience has been more than worthwhile. I have learned so much from my colleagues on that project, including Talia Stroud, Josh Tucker, Pablo Barberá, Taylor Brown, and Adriana Crespo Tenorio. And the hours I spent each week with Magdalena Wojcieszak, Jaime Settle, and Brendan Nyhan have been a highlight of the past three years. Each of them has not only inspired me to be a better researcher but also to find genuine joy in the research process.

I am lucky enough to have a family full of social scientists to help me with proofreading, thinking through thorny problems, and reassurance throughout a fraught process. Thanks to my father, Stuart Thorson, my mother, Kristi Andersen, and my brilliant sister, Kjerstin Thorson.

In addition to spanning three jobs, this book has also spanned three children. Sabine, Louis, and Cleo: thank you for being walking examples of faulty inductive reasoning, and more importantly for being such wonderful people. And to Stephan Stohler—you are the funniest, kindest person I know, and life with you makes everything better, including writing books.

1
Introduction

Misperceptions that matter

"Sharon" works part-time as a school administrator in rural Virginia. She identifies as a Democrat, though admits she does not follow politics closely. When I interviewed her, Sharon talked to me about the issues most important to her. Near the top of her list was the national debt. In particular, she expressed concern over the "fact" that the United States owed most of its debt to China. "They could take our stuff, our natural resources," Sharon told me. "They could demand that we give them stuff like that." To Sharon, China's majority ownership of U.S. debt posed a serious risk to national security: the threat of China "collecting" on its debt loomed much larger for her than concerns about healthcare or the environment.

Sharon is factually incorrect. Foreign entities own around a third of U.S. debt, and China owns just 8%. The majority of U.S. debt is owed to institutions within the United States, including U.S. citizens, mutual funds, and the Federal Reserve. But Sharon is far from alone in her misperception: about seven in ten Americans think that China owns the majority of U.S. debt, and many of them share Sharon's concern that China will "collect" by repossessing American property.

The false belief that China owns most of the national debt is one of many misperceptions about U.S. policy that together form what I call the *invented state*. Others include the belief that undocumented immigrants are eligible for food stamps and that there are no federal limits on welfare benefits. These misperceptions have a common thread. They are false beliefs not about political actors (e.g., Barack Obama's birthplace) nor about social and economic conditions (e.g., the unemployment rate), but rather about existing government policy. The concept of the "invented state" draws on Suzanne Mettler's observation that much of what the government does is "submerged," or invisible to ordinary citizens (Mettler 2011). This book makes two main claims: first, that this invisibility provides a fertile ground for misperceptions about existing government policy to flourish, and second, that correcting those misperceptions can profoundly change political attitudes.

While the precise contours of the invented state vary across individuals and across time, the factors that create it, including the media's tendency to ignore existing policy and the human drive to construct inferences, are consistent. This book identifies some of the misperceptions that make up the invented state as well as offering an explanation of how policy misperceptions arise, why they shape attitudes, and how they can be corrected.

This chapter explains how the invented state fits into the ongoing conversation about the role of misperceptions in democratic functioning. I argue that false beliefs pose the greatest threat to citizen competence when they lead people to hold attitudes or behave differently than they would behave if fully informed, and misperceptions about existing policy are especially likely to distort opinions in this way.

Political knowledge and democratic functioning

When are misperceptions a problem?

In our ideal of a functioning democracy, citizens base their preferences on a relatively accurate understanding of the world around them, and then politicians respond to those preferences (Kuklinski et al. 2000).[1] But this is a rather vague ideal, and translating it into measurable standards has generated a long and often contentious debate over exactly how much political knowledge is sufficient for effective democratic functioning (Fiorina 1981; Delli Carpini and Keeter 1996; Lau and Redlawsk 2001; Kuklinski and Quirk 2001). In response to this debate, Althaus (2006) suggests that holding citizens to an unreachably high standard of knowledge is not only impossible in practice but also reflects a fundamental misunderstanding of normative democratic theory: "For most of recorded history, the ignorance of ordinary people was therefore more of a 'given' than a 'crisis'... The problem of an ill-informed citizenry is a counterfeit crisis born of misunderstanding" (Althaus 2006, 91–96).

But if the answer to "how much do citizens need to know" is not simply "the more the better," then what exactly is it? Lupia (2015) offers a path out of this conundrum by suggesting that the critical question is not how much citizens need to know, but rather how this knowledge directly affects their behavior. Citizens are competent if their knowledge allows them to make decisions in line with their underlying preferences (Mansbridge 1983). Looking at knowledge through the lens of competence means that not all misperceptions (or ignorance) are inherently a threat to democratic functioning (Lupia et al. 1998). A person, or even wide swaths of the public, can be uninformed or misinformed without it affecting their competence.

For example, about 20% of Americans believe that Barack Obama was born outside of the United States. This widely held misperception persisted even after Obama's long-form birth certificate offered definitive proof that he was born in Hawaii (Berinsky 2023). This is on its face startling: millions of Americans believe something that is deeply false, even in the face of compelling evidence to the contrary. But the framework of competence pushes us to consider not just the magnitude of a misperception but also whether it distorts attitudes. And there is little evidence that believing Obama was born outside the U.S. led people to change their attitudes. Rather, the choice to believe the "birther" conspiracy is a direct product of those attitudes, including racism, dislike of Obama, and conservatism (Pasek, Stark, et al. 2015). The misperception, while troubling for a range of reasons, may not actually be a substantial threat to the competence of those who hold it.[2]

In this book, I argue that we should focus on the misperceptions that pose a direct threat to competence. Applying this standard could change how academics and journalists go about designing and implementing interventions to correct misperceptions. Currently, both academic and public attention tends to focus on the misperceptions that are the most novel, appalling, or divisive. Frequently, this category includes those that are sharply divided along partisan lines (e.g., false beliefs about Obama's birthplace).

However, when we see that a particular misperception is strongly associated with partisanship, this association should raise a red flag about its potential *causal* impact on attitudes. If Democrats are the only ones who falsely believe that the economy tanked during the first two years of Trump's presidency, then perhaps their partisan identity is the underlying cause of both their dislike of Trump and their false belief, rather than the false belief causing the dislike. The following section outlines the role of partisanship in shaping factual beliefs (and misperceptions), and explores why some types of factual beliefs may be less subject to partisan bias than others.

How partisanship shapes beliefs

People learn about the political world from a range of sources, including their experiences, the media, and their social interactions. Then, they draw on this knowledge to inform their attitudes. Partisanship complicates the relationship between facts and opinions in several ways.

Across a range of issues, Democrats and Republicans hold markedly divergent sets of factual beliefs. They offer different estimates of the COVID mortality rate (Robbett and Matthews 2020), hold different sets of beliefs around healthcare policy (Berinsky 2017), and perceive the economy differently (Prior et al. 2015). The media have devoted a great deal of attention to these differences, often featuring alarmist headlines like the *Economist*'s 2016 cover story "The Post-Truth World" (Economist 2016). Indeed, in 2016, the *Oxford English Dictionary* named "post-truth" its "word of the year," citing the increasing power of emotional partisan attachment to shape factual beliefs (Keane 2016).

While partisanship is undeniably a powerful force in creating our understanding of the political world, treating people's beliefs as *only* a product of partisan identity is as reductive and misleading as treating them as purely a product of objective rationality. Achen and Bartels (2017, 296) succinctly describe the average citizen's factual beliefs as "constructed mostly of folk wisdom and partisan surmise, with a trace element of reality." Much of the recent literature on information (and misinformation) has focused on the role of "partisan surmise," but much less attention has been paid to understanding how the relative amounts of "folk wisdom" and "reality" change depending on the person, the issue, and even the type of factual belief.

The extent to which partisanship shapes beliefs varies by person (with strong partisans generally relying more heavily on partisan cues) and by issue (with more "politicized" issues being more subject to partisan distortion). Stronger partisans are both more able to access partisan cues and more likely to construct beliefs in a way that protects their partisan identity (Lodge and Taber 2013). Arceneaux and Vander Wielen (2017) also posit that the extent to which individuals allow partisanship to color their attitudes and beliefs is partly a function of their underlying personality traits.

In addition, not all issues are equally tied to partisan identity. Empirically, this means that factual beliefs about highly politicized issues may diverge along party lines more than factual beliefs about less politicized issues. Partisan heuristics are more available for some issues than for others and are especially salient when issues have become highly politicized (Dowling et al. 2020; Nyhan and Reifler 2010).

Finally, the extent to which partisanship shapes a particular factual belief may depend on the nature of the fact, including its level of abstraction. Many studies measuring partisan bias in factual perceptions focus on "performance" indicators and ask participants to estimate seemingly objective quantities like the unemployment rate. For example, Achen and Bartels (2006) calculate the relative impact of partisanship versus "objective reality" in shaping beliefs about a range of dynamic economic indicators like the budget deficit and inflation. Similarly, Bartels (2002) examines the impact of partisanship on ten different factual beliefs, each of which have an explicit temporal dimension (e.g., participants are asked to estimate whether unemployment has risen or fallen, whether spending on public schools has increased or decreased, and whether inflation has gone up or down). Across these and many other studies asking about performance measures (Evans and Andersen 2006; Prior et al. 2015; Tilley and Hobolt 2011; Evans and Pickup 2010), partisanship strongly shapes participants' estimates.

All of these measures assess how well citizens understand the *outcomes* of policies rather than the policies themselves. There are good reasons to believe that outcome beliefs are important. Evaluating outcomes is cognitively easier than evaluating the complex policies that led to those outcomes, making these outcome beliefs the foundation for retrospective voting (Healy and Malhotra 2013). However, outcome measures are particularly sensitive to partisan bias because their time-sensitive aspect cues people to take into consideration the party in power (Gerber and Huber 2010). Precisely because they are measures of performance, they are implicit referendums on the current government (indeed, this is what makes them so valuable for retrospective voting), and so respondents automatically assess them through a partisan lens (Bisgaard 2019).

Beliefs about performance are only one aspect of political knowledge that shapes competence (Delli Carpini and Keeter 1996). People also hold factual beliefs about who falls into different tax brackets and who is in charge of collecting their garbage—in other words, beliefs about what policy actually does rather than about its outcomes. There are several reasons why partisanship may have a smaller effect on shaping beliefs about *existing* policy compared to beliefs about policy outcomes. First, the "party in power" heuristic is less relevant when understanding or evaluating long-standing policies (e.g. Social Security). Second, because news coverage of politics is biased toward novelty and change (Patterson 2013), people may have fewer opportunities to learn where their party stands on a policy not currently in the news. Of course, facts about current policy are not entirely immune to partisan inference (Udana 2018). Still, while Achen and Bartels (2017) are inarguably correct that "partisan surmise" plays a large (and potentially growing) role in factual perceptions (and misperceptions), there are a wide range of issues for which partisanship is not particularly useful as a heuristic for belief formation.

What kinds of false beliefs threaten competence?

Beliefs, both true and false, affect how and when citizens exercise political power to help create a world aligned with their values and preferences. One way for people to exercise this power is through voting, but factual beliefs shape the political world in other, more subtle ways as well. What people know (or think they know) about politics affects how they discuss politics with their friends, what stories they click on in their Facebook feed, and whether they choose to vote in the first place—and all of these in turn shape both who is elected and what policies they enact (Southwell et al. 2018; Kuklinski et al. 2001; Delli Carpini and Keeter 1996).

Discussions of information effects in politics sometimes implicitly assume that the opposite of knowledge is ignorance. However, misperceptions may pose a much greater threat to citizen competence and thus to democratic functioning: holding false beliefs "can lead to collective preferences that differ significantly from those that would exist if people were adequately informed" (Kuklinski et al. 2000, 792). Consider Citizen X, a strongly anti-abortion voter. Citizen X must choose between Candidate A and Candidate B but does not know the two candidates' stances on abortion. Citizen X's ignorance might affect her actions in several ways. She might seek out information on the candidates' positions, decide to rely on the two candidates' partisan affiliations as a shortcut, or abstain from voting altogether. Her ignorance will also affect what she does *not* do. She will likely not tell her friends about the candidates' stances on abortion (since she does not know what those stances are) or write an angry letter about them to the local paper. If she does choose to vote, she will not explicitly base her vote on the candidates' position on abortion.

Now, consider Citizen Y. Citizen Y is also strongly anti-abortion, but unlike Citizen X, Citizen Y holds a misperception about the one of the candidates. Specifically, he incorrectly believes that Candidate A is pro-choice, when in reality Candidate A is strongly pro-life. Citizen Y is unlikely to seek out additional information about candidates' positions on the issue because he believes that he already has this information. His misperception might shape his preferences, making him more likely to cast a vote for Candidate B over Candidate A. It might also shape his behavior; increasing the likelihood he discusses the issue with friends, thereby potentially spreading the misinformation to more people (Weeks and Garrett 2014). When misperceptions inform people's attitudes and behavior, it can compromise both citizen competence and democratic responsiveness.

Because voting is the primary way that citizens translate their preferences into political outcomes, misperceptions about candidates (as in the previous example) intuitively feel like a major threat to voter competence. We worry that false beliefs about candidates will lead voters to act in a way that runs counter to their own self-interest. Many of us have felt the frustration of trying to convince someone that the so-called factual belief they hold about a political candidate is wrong. These arguments tend to be over high-profile factual disputes that break down along partisan lines, with Democrats and Republicans fervently defending their versions of the truth, from whether George Bush orchestrated the September 11 attacks (he did not) and whether Sarah Palin banned books in the Wasilla library (she did not) to whether Barack Obama was born in the United States (he was) and whether Hillary Clinton had a terminal illness (she did not). These highly partisan misperceptions also took center stage in the 2016 election, when "fake news" stories on Facebook spread misinformation about Hillary Clinton and Donald Trump (Silverman 2016; Alcott and Gentzkow 2017).

Is this intuition justified? Do misperceptions about candidates lead people to vote in ways that run counter to their interests? Substantial academic research suggests that while this outcome is possible, it is surprisingly rare. Instead of shaping attitudes, these highly politicized misperceptions are largely the product of attitudes—namely, partisan identity. Democrats and Republicans seek out and believe information that reinforces their existing opinions, even when that information is unsupported by fact (Flynn et al. 2017; Swire et al. 2017). For the most part, these candidate-centered misperceptions emerge from explicit misinformation (Berinsky 2023; Weeks and Southwell 2010) and are extremely difficult to correct (Garrett and

Weeks 2013; Nyhan and Reifler 2010) because they are deeply intertwined with partisan identity. Thus, rather than leading people to vote contrary to their interest, candidate misperceptions tend to be direct expressions of that interest. While candidate misperceptions feel intuitively problematic (and viscerally annoying), a greater normative threat may come from a type of misperception that has received far less attention but is extraordinarily common: false beliefs about policy.

How policy misperceptions threaten competence

In Chapter 2, I use interviews to elicit factual beliefs about politics. A common thread in these interviews, confirmed across several representative surveys, is that misperceptions about existing policy, from Social Security to welfare to taxes, are surprisingly widespread. This finding forms the foundation for the rest of the book, which outlines both how these false beliefs emerge and the effects of correcting them.

Survey questions that measure factual beliefs about existing policy, which I refer to throughout the book as "policy-current" questions, are relatively rare. For example, between 2000 and 2013, policy-current questions comprised just 12% of the political knowledge items on the American National Election Survey. Most of the questions were about civics-related topics (e.g., the number of justices on the Supreme Court or the length of a president's term) (Barabas et al. 2014). Civics questions are asked more frequently on surveys for good reason: this type of knowledge is highly predictive of normatively desirable behaviors, including several forms of political participation (Delli Carpini and Keeter 1996).

While civics knowledge is associated with participation, it may be less directly relevant to the question of citizen competence (Gilens 2001, Lupia 2006). In contrast, policy knowledge directly affects citizens' ability to connect their values to specific policy outcomes (Alvarez and Brehm 2002; Gilens 2001). Misperceptions about existing policy can impede citizen competence by altering priorities, impeding debate, and distorting preferences.

The government operates via inputs (in the form of tax dollars) and outputs (policies and laws). Democratic accountability requires that citizens be able to evaluate these inputs and outputs and hold legislators responsible for them. Elections are referendums not only on candidates but also on the policies that they have enacted or propose to change. But debates over what the government *should* do are meaningless unless voters have a shared belief about what the government *is* doing. Widely held misperceptions about policy threaten citizens' ability to hold their elected officials accountable and prioritize their desired policy outcomes (Hochschild and Einstein 2015). For example, Sharon's belief that China owned the national debt led her to prioritize that issue over others that mattered to her. Citizen attention is limited (Baumgartner and Jones 2010), and false beliefs can direct attention away from some issues and toward others. Indeed, politicians can strategically use misinformation to influence the public's priorities: for example, during the 2016 election, Donald Trump falsely stated that the murder rate was the highest it had been in 47 years (Jacobson 2017). Concern about crime in the U.S. rose to a 15-year high in 2016 (Davis 2016), with eight in ten Trump voters describing crime as a "very serious problem" (Francovic 2016).

Misperceptions also hinder political debate, both at the elite and interpersonal levels. In many political debates, people have shared goals (e.g., lower crime rates) but disagree over what policies can best help reach those goals. A shared understanding of the policy that currently exists is a critical foundation for productive deliberation. Most existing policies are a direct product of at least some political compromise. Therefore, they will often be more palatable to both sides than any novel policy proposed by either side, and can thus be a useful baseline for evaluating new ideas (Fishkin 2011; Flynn et al. 2017). To give a concrete example, if someone incorrectly believes that the U.S. does not check refugees' backgrounds before admitting them, then they may find any refugee policy reform that does not include background checks unacceptable—even though in reality, background checks have long been required for refugees.

Finally, the invented state may distort preferences, leading people to hold policy preferences that are different than they would hold if they were fully informed. Preference distortion is a common concern raised about the effects of political misinformation. For example, we might worry that someone who believed a false rumor that a candidate embezzled funds was less likely to vote for her, or someone who incorrectly thought that the Affordable Care Act (ACA) includes death panels was less likely to support it. Of course, both examples involve an explicit choice between two different potential outcomes: Candidate A versus Candidate B being elected, or the ACA passing versus failing. However, misperceptions can also reduce support for existing policy (e.g., the false belief that SNAP benefits are available to undocumented immigrants might lower a person's support for the program).

Indeed, in Chapter 6 I show correcting common misperceptions increases support for existing policy across five different issue areas.

The creation of the invented state

Where do policy misperceptions come from? Some are attributable to explicit misinformation. For example, many Americans came to believe that the 2010 Affordable Care Act contained "death panels" that would result in seriously ill people being denied necessary medical treatment—a false belief based on misleading statements from conservative pundits (Nyhan 2010). However, exposure to misinformation is not the only source of misperceptions. Many false beliefs arise not because people are exposed to "fake news" or politicians' lies, but because they lack the necessary information to make sense of a complicated political world, and their efforts to "fill in the blank" lead them to incorrect conclusions. The increasingly fragmented media environment exacerbates this situation; not only because misinformation can spread more easily (Kim and Kim 2019) but also because a surfeit of options can make it difficult for citizens to find the information they need to fully understand an issue (Bennett 1996b; Bradburn 2016).

Fundamentally, people come to hold misperceptions in much the same ways that they come to hold any factual belief about politics: they cobble together "pictures in their heads" based on personal experience, media coverage, and their assumptions and beliefs (Lippmann 1922). Most of what we know about politics, both correct and incorrect, comes not from direct, lived experience but through intermediaries. Civics textbooks inform us how the government works. The media tell us which issues matter and why. Politicians explain how our tax dollars were spent. We combine this (often incomplete and sometimes inaccurate) information with our experiences (and, of course, our own biases) to construct a set of beliefs about reality that may correspond only inexactly to the facts on the ground. Walter Lippmann, writing almost a century ago, warned that this mental process could lead us deeply astray:

> The casual fact, the creative imagination, the will to believe, and out of these three elements, a counterfeit of reality to which there was a violent instinctive response. For it is clear enough that under certain conditions men respond as powerfully to fictions as they do to realities, and that in many cases

they help to create the very fictions to which they respond . . . By fictions I do not mean lies. I mean a representation of the environment which is in lesser or greater degree made by man himself. (Lippmann 1922)

Lippmann describes three factors that, together, can create a compelling political "fiction." First, the "casual fact": the information a person has encountered about a given issue. When a person learns about an issue, it is usually not through a systematic and careful review, but rather through fragmented headlines and articles that often lack critical context and background information (Bennett 1996b; Jerit 2009). What is *not* said can be as important as what *is* said in creating misperceptions, especially given the relative dearth of substantive policy content compared to coverage of candidate strategy and other "horse race" stories (Faris et al. 2017). Even when the campaign season is over, media attention rarely turns to matters of established public policy, largely *because* it is established: there is little that is novel and thus deemed worthy of news coverage. As Mettler points out, the "policies of the submerged state have not been the subject of sustained and extensive partisan elite debate . . . The lack of much overt controversy over such policies discourages coverage by the news media, which largely follows elite cues and is drawn to dramatic conflict" (Mettler 2011, 54). One of the consequences of this lack of coverage is, as we might expect, ignorance—and indeed, Mettler finds that many citizens are substantially ignorant about much of what the U.S. government does. But this lack of coverage also creates a fertile ground for misperceptions.

The second factor, what Lippmann calls the "creative imagination," speaks to the inherent human drive to draw inferences from even the smallest piece of information. The mind is "a machine for jumping to conclusions" (Kahneman 2011), but the existence of systematic cognitive biases means that the conclusions that it jumps to are often very wrong (Wyer and Albarracín 2005). When trying to comprehend the issue of the national debt, for example, a person might automatically (and even unconsciously) employ a familiar metaphor: personal debt. Personal debt is usually owed to external companies like banks or credit card companies: entities that, if unpaid, will come to collect. But drawing these parallels with the national debt leads to erroneous inferences about to whom the national debt is owed and the consequences of a failure to pay.

The third factor answers the question of why Americans remain ignorant about some issues but form misperceptions about others. There are hundreds of issues that the media do not cover and about which the public knows little, from Argentinian trade agreements to licensing requirements for zookeepers. But most Americans probably do not hold false beliefs about exactly how much training a zookeeper needs before she is legally allowed to throw a fish to a seal. Why does a person form misperceptions around some issues but not others? I argue that the catalyst for the creation of misperceptions is what Lippmann called the "will to believe" —the desire to understand the issue at hand. Only when a person believes an issue to be important will they engage in the cognitive work necessary to form beliefs (either accurate or inaccurate) about it. Someone might come to believe an issue is important for a wide range of reasons, including self-interest, values, elite discourse, or even simply being asked a survey question. Regardless of the reason, people are more likely to spend time thinking (or, as social scientists call it, "engaging in cognitive elaboration") about issues that they deem to be important, and engaging in this cognitive elaboration increases the likelihood that they will, in Lippmann's words, "create the very fictions to which they respond." The "will to believe" is thus the final and necessary component for the creation of the invented state.

The invented state is problematic, and yet it also offers reasons for optimism about citizen competence and participation. The misperceptions that make up the invented state are largely created from citizens' struggle to understand issues that they believe are important. Insofar as we value citizens grappling with political issues, the existence of the invented state means that they are doing just that. Misperceptions may be more dangerous than ignorance in many ways, but they also demonstrate effort rather than apathy.

Organization of the Book

The first half of this book draws on a wide range of empirical approaches to describe the invented state and understand how it emerges, while the second half focuses on how it shapes attitudes and what can be done to dismantle it.

First, in Chapter 2, I identify some of the misperceptions that make up the invented state. I take a bottom-up approach, using a series of interviews to elicit some of the factual beliefs about policy underlying citizens' political attitudes and priorities. The misperceptions I identify in these interviews inform a representative panel survey that measures a range of policy misperceptions that are both widely held and strongly believed. In Chapter 3,

I describe how the media helps create the invented state—not, I argue, by spreading misinformation but by offering fragmented and incomplete coverage of many of the substantive policy issues that animate political debate. A content analysis demonstrates the dearth of policy-current information in news coverage. Chapter 4 solves the puzzle of why citizens remain ignorant about some issues and form misperceptions about others. The results of an experiment manipulating issue salience shows that citizens are more likely to form misperceptions about an issue when they believe that it matters, and the responses to open-ended questions illustrate how faulty inductive reasoning can create misperceptions.

In Chapter 5, I take on the question of why corrective information about policy *outcomes* often seems to have surprisingly small effects on attitudes. The answer, I suggest, is that people are especially prone to interpret information about policy outcomes through a partisan lens (e.g., by crediting their in-party or blaming the out-party). In contrast, information about existing policy is less shaped by partisan-driven motivated reasoning, making it potentially more likely to distort rather than reinforce attitudes. Chapter 6 offers empirical evidence that correcting misperceptions about existing policy also affects opinions, both by increasing support and by altering priorities.

Chapter 7 tackles the question of dismantling the invented state. I draw on data showing not only that policy misperceptions can be corrected but also that these corrections are remarkably long-lasting—even among people who originally expressed a great deal of confidence in their false beliefs. In addition, and contrary to popular opinion, people demonstrate a strong preference for news coverage of existing policy. Finally, Chapter 8 concludes by outlining the implications of this book for our understanding of democratic competence. I consider the extent to which different journalistic formats can address the information deficit that leads to misperceptions as well as describe interventions that can minimize misperceptions and maximize citizens' abilities to make informed decisions about politics.

2
The contours of the invented state

Chapter 1 introduced the concept of the "invented state": widespread misperceptions about public policy that could impede democratic functioning. This chapter uses a bottom-up approach to measure factual beliefs, with the goal of identifying commonly held misperceptions about existing policy.

The origins of misperceptions

When it comes to politics, just about everyone is wrong about something. You may not believe that former President Barack Obama is secretly Muslim, but perhaps you mistakenly think that judges in your town are elected, not appointed, or that crime rates in your state are much higher than they really are. All of these are political misperceptions, but they likely differ along several important dimensions, including how you came to hold them in the first place and the extent to which they are tied to your partisan identity. This section outlines some of the ways that misperceptions arise and argues that the varied origins of political misperceptions make them uniquely difficult to identify with survey research alone.

Explicit misinformation

Sometimes people come to hold misperceptions because they were exposed to misinformation. In 2009, 41% of Americans believed that the Affordable Care Act (ACA) included so-called death panels that would prevent the sick and elderly people from receiving necessary healthcare (CNN/ORC 2009). Brendan Nyhan (2010) shows that this misperception arose after a false claim by conservative pundit Betsy McCaughey was amplified and repeated by the media. Similarly, exposure to the type of "fake news" stories that spread during the 2016 election can also create misperceptions (Silverman 2016), although of course not everyone exposed to a piece of misinformation will believe it (Allcott and Gentzkow 2017).

Misperceptions that are directly caused by exposure to misinformation are relatively straightforward to identify, partly because there is a growing industry explicitly devoted to identifying false claims in elite political discourse. Fact-checking organizations routinely scan politicians' statements and campaign advertisements to identify misinformation, and many also tackle rumors that spread via emails and social media (Graves 2016; Amazeen 2016). The mission statement of the popular fact-checking website PolitiFact describes their mission as checking the claims of "elected officials, candidates, leaders of political parties, advocacy groups, political action committees, pundits, columnists, widely circulated chain emails, bloggers, political analysts, the hosts and guests of talk shows, and other members of the media" (Politifact 2017).

By asking survey questions about these false claims, researchers can attempt to measure the extent to which misinformation in the media has shaped the public's beliefs. But this approach paints an incomplete picture of the total universe of public misperceptions because fact-checking organizations focus almost entirely on finding and correcting misinformation (false information) rather than misperceptions (false beliefs) (Wilner 2016). And while some misperceptions do originate from exposure to misinformation, others stem from another source: individuals' unsuccessful (and often biased) attempts to make sense of an often-confusing political world.

Biased processing

In politics as in other areas, individuals' cognitive biases can lead them to make incorrect inferences about the world around them (Arceneaux 2012; Lau and Redlawsk 2001). Partisanship is a major cause of biased processing in the political world (Lodge and Taber 2013). As discussed in Chapter 1, many factual misperceptions are directly attributable to reliance on partisan heuristics. Factual questions that reflect on the party in power are especially susceptible to partisan influence: for example, Democrats are more likely to overestimate the unemployment rate when a Republican is in the White House (Achen and Bartels 2017).

However, not all biases are partisan in nature. About 15% of Americans believe over half of all U.S. spending goes to foreign aid (DiJulio and Brodie

2016), even though foreign aid makes up less than 1% of the budget. This misperception is driven partly by the availability heuristic: when estimating the size of a category, people tend to overestimate the size of categories that are vivid and easily accessible (Kahneman 2011), and foreign aid is more memorable than (for example) tax breaks for homeowners. Thus, while the misperception is created through biased processing, the bias is not partisan in nature: indeed, Democrats and Republicans are equally likely to incorrectly overestimate the amount spent on foreign aid (CBS News 2011). Chapter 4 discusses in more detail how cognitive biases contribute to the creation of misperceptions.

Biases (either partisan or not) can be exacerbated by the information environment. To return to the foreign aid example, most politicians may stop short of explicitly lying about the percent of the budget that goes to foreign aid, but many implicitly argue that the amount is too large. For example, in 2017, White House Office of Management and Budget director Mick Mulvaney argued that cuts in foreign aid would enable a $54 billion expansion of the military budget. "The overriding message is fairly straightforward: less money spent overseas means more money spent here," said Mulvaney (Shepardson 2017). In reality, the international aid budget at that time was only around $34 million (OECD 2016), so even cutting the entire amount would have been insufficient to fund the proposed expansion.

Such "implied" misinformation is rarely noted by fact-checking organizations but can have real effects on beliefs (Rich and Zaragoza 2016). When media coverage of the 1998–1999 debate over Social Security used words like "bankrupt," citizens who read that coverage were more likely to incorrectly believe that Social Security would run out of money completely if no changes to the program were made (Jerit and Barabas 2006). While this media coverage was not explicitly endorsing or repeating misinformation, the language it used, combined with a lack of accurate information about the program, had the direct consequence of increasing misperceptions.

Political elites may strategically use implied misinformation to shift public opinion while also avoiding the scrutiny of fact-checking organizations. Indeed, this approach may be even more effective as some fact-checkers shift their focus away from fact-checking politicians and toward combating online misinformation (Graves and Mantzarlis 2020). Fact-checkers may also opt to avoid fact-checking political rhetoric that is merely misleading rather than straightforwardly wrong out of worries about being perceived as biased.

Why do the origins of misperceptions matter?

Where political misperceptions come from matters for several reasons. First, from a practical perspective, understanding the origin of misperceptions can help inform effective interventions to correct them and/or stop their spread. Second, tracing the origin of misperceptions can provide insight into their potential downstream effects on attitudes. And finally (and most importantly for this chapter), understanding where misperceptions come from is critical to identifying them in the first place.

Figure 2.1 presents a simplified framework of two of the major factors that generate political misperceptions. The x axis represents the "internal-external" dimension, which assesses whether a misperception is attributable to biased reasoning, explicit misinformation, or a combination of both. The y axis shows the extent to which a misperception is aligned with partisan identity.

The misperceptions on the right side of the graph are traceable to explicit misinformation like online rumors, "fake news," and false statements from elites. Many of these misperceptions have received a great deal of attention from the media, and much academic work on political misperceptions has focused on those in the upper right-hand quadrant: highly politicized false beliefs directly caused by explicit misinformation. Examples include

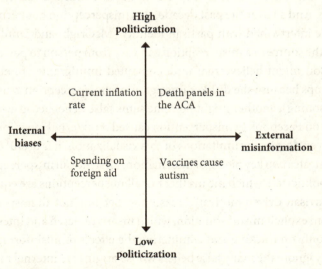

Figure 2.1 Origins of political misperceptions

death panels in the ACA (Nyhan 2010), President Obama's birthplace and religion (Hollander 2010; Weeks and Southwell 2010), and the size of the crowd at President Trump's inauguration (Schaffner and Luks 2018). Those in the bottom right-hand corner are attributable to explicit misinformation, but their association with partisan identity is currently minimal. The belief that vaccines are harmful is a particularly salient example of this type of misperception (Pew Research Center 2017).

The misperceptions on the left side of the graph are created largely by biased reasoning processes, which means that they cannot be identified simply by tracing the effects of elite discourse, "fake news," or online rumors. For the false beliefs in the upper left-hand corner, this biased reasoning is often heavily influenced by partisan identity—for example, partisans' tendency to overestimate inflation and underestimate employment when the opposing party is in power. The misperceptions in the lower left-hand corner are created by biases unrelated to partisanship, like the availability heuristic (as in the case of overestimating the percent spent on foreign aid), ignorance of base rates, and anchoring (Kahneman 2011).

While Figure 2.1 is a helpful visual shortcut, it is also an oversimplification in several ways. First, the extent to which a fact is politicized can change quickly. For example, when the issue of climate change first emerged, attitudes about it (and belief in its existence) were not clearly divided along partisan lines. Over time, elite discourse about the issue became more polarized, with many conservatives explicitly expressing doubt about the reality of global warming. And so over the past decade, this misperception has become more and more intertwined with partisan identity (McCright and Dunlap 2011). Second, the source of a misperception can vary from person to person. While one person might believe that undocumented immigrants are eligible for food stamps because she dislikes immigrants (a misperception caused by biased reasoning), another might hold the same false belief because her friend posted it on Facebook (a misperception caused by external misinformation).

However, despite the limitations of this visualization, it is useful because it communicates two key pieces of information. First, not all misperceptions are equally politicized, which means that not all misperceptions are equally subject to partisan-driven motivated reasoning. Second, not all misperceptions come from explicit misinformation, which means research and interventions focused only on tracking and eliminating the effects of misinformation will inevitably ignore the many false beliefs whose origins are internal rather than external.

The invented state is fundamentally about *policy* misperceptions, but Figure 2.1 does not explicitly address the substantive content of the misperception. This omission is deliberate, because policy misperceptions can fall along any of those dimensions. A misperception about policy can be politicized or not, and it can be a product of internal biases or external misinformation. However, as I argue in this chapter and in more detail in Chapter 3, many widely held policy misperceptions fall into the lower left-hand quadrant—they are relatively less politicized and more likely to be a product of biased reasoning than other types of political misperceptions.

Because policy misperceptions can arise both from visible, explicit misinformation and from invisible, complex cognitive processes (as well as from the interaction between these two factors), measuring them poses several challenges. Most existing studies of political misperceptions have focused on misperceptions that stem directly from misinformation, such as the belief that former President Obama was born outside the United States or that the pope endorsed Donald Trump (Nyhan 2017; Allcott and Gentzkow 2017). Such misinformation is relatively straightforward to identify, especially since fact-checking organizations and media outlets keep careful track of misinformation spread by politicians, online rumoring, or misleading advertisements (Graves 2016). But misperceptions that are not directly traceable to explicit misinformation are more difficult to observe and measure.

An interview approach to eliciting factual beliefs

Pairing interviews with surveys to identify factual beliefs has a long history in health (Bauman and Adair 1992), education (Desimone and Le Floch 2004), and marketing (Steenkamp and Van Trijp 1997), but this approach is less common in political science. However, interviews can provide unique insights into how citizens conceptualize the political world. In *Talking Politics*, William Gamson analyzes interpersonal conversations about politics to better understand how individuals "negotiate meaning" —in other words, how they transform the fragmented information environment into meaningful political attitudes (Gamson 1992). Similarly, Kathy Cramer shows how interpersonal political discussion shapes political opinions, often by helping people connect abstract political information to their own social identities and communities (Walsh 2004). Gamson and Cramer both analyze interpersonal conversations about politics with the goal of understanding how people come to hold a particular set of political *attitudes*. In contrast, the goal of this book is to better understand how people come to believe particular *facts*.

Fundamentally, facts matter because they help people connect their values with their political behavior (Lupia 2015, 219). Which facts matter for which people will depend on what their values are. And thus rather than taking a top-down approach that assumes the importance of a particular set of facts, I take a bottom-up approach that allows people to identify the facts (or misperceptions) that matter to their opinions and preferences. The goal is to avoid the problem succinctly summarized by Lupia (2006), in which academics' own beliefs about what facts matter inform how they assess public knowledge:

> Most political-knowledge questions are not derived from a replicable or transparent logic about how their answers bear on a voter's ability to make decisions of a particular quality in the voting booth. Instead, the questions are generated by a worldview that is shared by a select set of academics, journalists, and politicos, but few others.

In addition, because the beliefs that people spontaneously articulate in conversation are highly accessible, they may be more likely to exert a causal impact on attitudes and behavior (Kaplan and Fishbein 1969; Van Ittersum et al. 2007). Thus, as a first step toward identifying the factual misperceptions people hold about policy (and potentially those that shape their attitudes about those policies), I employ open-ended interviews to elicit subjects' factual beliefs without preconceived assumptions about what facts "should be" important to them.

Interview protocol

Along with a research assistant, I conducted 40 phone interviews over the course of the spring and summer of 2014. Participants for the phone interviews were recruited from Craigslist. While Craigslist is used with some frequency to recruit participants for medical studies (Ramo et al. 2010; Worthen 2014), it is less common in the social sciences. The advertisement, following best practices established by past researchers (Worthen 2014), was posted in the "volunteer" section with the headline "Phone Interview with a University Researcher, $15." The advertisement itself said that adults were being recruited for phone interviews "as part of a study about jobs and today's economy," the interview would last about 20 minutes, and those who participated would receive a $15 Target or Walmart gift card as compensation. Interested participants were directed to a brief online survey and told that not everyone who filled out the survey would be selected to participate. In order to maximize geographic diversity, the advertisement was placed in 38 areas (see Table 2.1) selected at random from the 414 total areas in which Craigslist had a presence in 2014.

The online survey consisted of a consent form, demographic questions, and an open-ended question asking participants what they perceived to be the most pressing issue facing the United States today. A total of 528 people took the online survey. Of those, 50 were selected to be contacted for an interview. Participants were selected with the goal of creating a sample that varied by age, sex, race, income, education, and political party. Selected participants were emailed to schedule an interview time. Forty phone interviews were successfully completed, ranging in length from 10 to 25 minutes. All interviews were recorded (with respondents' permission) and later transcribed.

About a third of the participants identified as Democrats, a third as Independents, and a third as Republicans, which is reflective of the U.S. population more broadly. The sample was better educated than the general public: 45% reported completing at least four years of college, compared

Table 2.1 Advertised Craigslist areas

Bemidji, MN	Cedar Rapids, IA	Charleston, SC
Charlottesville, VA	Corpus Christi, TX	Dallas/Fort Worth, TX
Del Rio/Eagle Pass, TX	Duluth/Superior, MN	Eastern Montana
Flagstaff/Sedona, AZ	Flint, MI	Florida Keys
Ft Myers/SW Florida	Gadsden-Anniston, AL	Green Bay, WI
Hanford-Corcoran, CA	Harrisburg, PA	Hickory/Lenoir, NC
Houma, LA	Iowa City, IA	Lansing, MI
Nashville, TN	Mason City, IA	Memphis, TN
Plattsburgh-Adirondacks, NY	New Haven, CT	Northern WI
Salem, OR	Pueblo, CO	Rockford, IL
South Dakota	Santa Fe/Taos, NM	Skagit/Island/SJI, WA
Zanesville/Cambridge, OH	Southeast Alaska	Wichita Falls, TX

to 30% of Americans. The full demographic breakdown of the sample is listed in Table 2.2

Interview subjects were first told that they could decline to answer any question and then that the goal of the interview was to better understand what Americans think about politics. Casually embedded in the introduction was the statement that "the media do not always do a good job of giving people the information they need about political issues." This sentence was deliberately inserted to help subjects feel more comfortable stating if or when they did not know something, thereby reducing the likelihood that they would construct factual answers solely to satisfy the interviewer. The

Table 2.2 Demographics of interview subjects ($N = 40$)

	Percent	N
Age		
18–24	10.0	4
25–34	27.5	11
35–44	17.5	7
45–54	25.0	10
55+	20.0	8
Education		
High school	17.5	7
Some college	37.5	15
4 years of college	32.5	13
Post-graduate	12.5	5
Income		
Less than 30k	37.5	15
30–50k	27.5	11
50–70k	22.5	9
70k+	7.5	3
Race		
White	75	30
Black	10	4
Other	15	6
Party		
Democrat	30	12
Republican	32.5	13
Independent	12.5	11
No preference	27.6	5

conversation started by asking about the issue that the respondent had indicated in the survey as their "most important issue." These included the economy, healthcare, and immigration.

After discussing this most important issue, the conversation moved to other questions about the U.S. debt, social welfare programs, size of government, unemployment, immigration, entitlement programs, and taxes. These policy areas were chosen because they frequently top the results of Gallup's "most important problem" survey.[1]

The interviewers asked about the participants' general thoughts and experiences with these issues. In some cases, to encourage factual assertions, the participants were asked how they would explain a certain topic to a child or what information they wished more people knew about an issue. While the topics included in the interviews remained consistent, the wording of the questions varied according to the flow of the interview. The participants were not asked specific factual questions or "quizzed" in any way. Rather, they were encouraged (but not required) to include factual assertions as part of their larger discussions about politics and policy. At the end of the interviews, interviewees were given the opportunity to mention any issues important to them that had not previously been discussed.

Misperceptions elicited in interviews

Each interview was subsequently transcribed and then analyzed for either direct or indirect factual claims. It is important to note that because this book focuses on misperceptions, the discussion below largely ignores the many correct factual assertions made in the interview. On many issues, ranging from unemployment policy to Social Security, interviewees showed an impressive grasp of complex policies. On the whole, respondents were also very willing to state when they did not know something. Indeed, respondents were often reluctant to make factual assertions concerning issues about which they perceived they knew little. This reluctance suggests that the factual statements they *did* feel comfortable sharing were held with some degree of confidence rather than merely answers given to satisfy interviewer demand. Below, I summarize the most frequently mentioned misperceptions around six general areas: the national debt, social welfare programs, immigration, entitlement programs, government spending, and taxes.[2]

National debt

The interviews probed respondents' beliefs about the causes and consequences of the national debt. Many respondents expressed concern about the issue, and several focused on China's ownership of U.S. debt and the potential for China to exercise an outsize influence in U.S. affairs. As Andrea put it, "We owe China our backside because they've lended to us." People also expressed concern about the interest on the national debt. Raul described it as "digging ourselves into a hole," stating: "Once you have mounting debt and interest that comes on top of the debt, it's almost impossible to get out of that hole." Melissa agreed, stating that "we'll be paying such high interest rates that we might as well be bankrupt."

Social welfare programs

In discussing programs like welfare, food stamps, and even unemployment, a common theme emerged that cut across party lines: the assumption that most beneficiaries were adults who used the programs for years, if not a lifetime. Alison strongly supported these programs in general, saying that "we should have systems . . . if someone has an unexpected illness or loses their job, becomes unemployed, loses their health insurance, or becomes a single parent." But she went on to succinctly summarize a common concern: "Those programs have gone from temporary solutions that maybe last six months, a year, two years, at the most five years and now they've just become a way of life." The belief that welfare benefits were unlimited worried Sean. "They count on that check, they know it's going to come, so they don't put their minds to use to become something better." Almost exclusively, discussion around these programs centered on adults: only one interviewee mentioned that children also benefit from these programs.

Spending

When asked about the government size and efficiency, a common complaint was government size—several respondents stated that government was simply too big. In addition, especially among self-identified Democrats, people objected to what they perceived as too much spending on the military. Said Lianne, "While supporting the military is a worthy pursuit, supporting the war with such rigor while there are a lot of things at home that need to be taken care of . . . I think it's criminal."

Immigration

Immigration was a concern for many respondents, who expressed concern for the burden that undocumented immigrants were placing on the system. Mark complained, "They've got more rights than we as Americans do." One respondent expressed worries that large families might overwhelm the education system, and two mentioned undocumented immigrants' use of food stamps.

Entitlement programs

Interview subjects were also asked about their understanding of programs like Social Security and Medicare. Most participants had a roughly accurate idea of how both programs worked. However, several respondents believed that Social Security was akin to a savings account in which people could deposit money as they worked, and then withdraw this money upon retirement. As Jacob described the system, "When you are not able to work or you retire . . . all the money you put away while you were working, get[s] paid back to you." And while most respondents were aware that Medicare was a healthcare program for older people, others were uncertain or incorrect as to how it actually functioned.

Taxes

When asked about taxes, interviewees were concerned about two groups not paying their fair share: the wealthy and corporations. "Taxes on things or people that are making a lot more money than anybody else should be raised," said Lianne. Connie agreed: "You constantly hear about companies that don't pay taxes," and Taylor commented, "Billionaires paying a lower percentage of their income than people who work for them at a much lower wage, that's a broken system."

Several patterns were common across all six issue areas. First, respondents rarely offered specific numerical estimates for quantities like unemployment, the national debt, or tax brackets. Instead, they used phrases like "a lot" or offered comparative assessments (e.g., the United States spends more on the military than on healthcare).

This tendency suggests not that people are innumerate, but that their political beliefs take the form of broad concepts and comparisons rather than specific numbers. In addition, despite the prevalence of performance indicators (e.g., the unemployment rate) in research on factual perceptions

(Bartels 2002; Bisgaard 2019), few respondents mentioned these indicators explicitly. In general, their discussions of policy outcomes tended to focus more on what groups or people get which benefits: for example, who is eligible for entitlement programs or who is taxed more or less.

A number of misperceptions were mentioned by both Democrats and Republicans, and at times to support very different policy positions. For example, while one Democratic respondent cited the (incorrect) fact that TANF offered lifetime benefits to argue that the program needed more resources, a Republican respondent mentioned the same misperception to justify his opinion that the program should be eliminated.

Finally, it is important to note that many of the statements made by interview subjects were not explicitly false statements. For example, several people asserted that the government is "too big." This statement is, of course, a matter of opinion and does not directly imply that the respondents making it hold any misperceptions. However, the observation is a clue that government size *matters* to many people, and they may hold factual beliefs about its size that are worth further investigation. The interview approach does not generate a neat set of misperceptions, rather it produces a constellation of opinions, half-truths, and assertions that can serve as a window into false beliefs that people might hold. To assess their prevalence more systematically requires a different approach.

Measuring the scope of misperceptions

These interview data offer an initial glimpse at the "invented state" that is independent from researchers' assumptions about what people do or should know about issues. However, the inferences we can draw from these data are limited by the fact that the interview subjects were a small and unrepresentative sample. Therefore, I use a representative survey to gauge the prevalence of some of the misperceptions elicited in the interview study in the general public. The survey was administered as a module of the 2014 Cooperative Congressional Election Study (CCES), a stratified national sample of registered and unregistered adults weighted to create a nationally representative sample of U.S. adults. The panel survey ($N = 1,000$) was administered in two waves, one in mid-October and one in mid-November.[3] Two-thirds of the sample answered the 12 factual questions in the first wave, and the rest answered them in the second wave.[4] Both the format and the content of these questions were directly informed by the results of the interviews described in the previous section.

Question Format

The questions were introduced with the following text: "You will be presented with several pairs of statements. In each pair, one statement is true and one statement is false. Please select the statement that you think is most correct. If you are not sure, take a moment to think and then make your best guess." The full set of questions is presented in Table 2.3. Immediately after the participant selected an answer, a follow-up question popped up on the same screen asking whether they were "very confident," "somewhat confident," or "not confident at all" in their answer.

This question format differs in several ways from measures of political knowledge, which usually take either a multiple-choice, fill-in-the-blank, open-ended, or true-false format (Sturgis et al. 2007; Robison 2014). The format was informed by the results of the interviews and specifically designed to address some of the most common challenges in assessing political knowledge: innumeracy, acquiescence bias, and guessing.

The first issue, innumeracy, describes the challenges of answering questions that deal directly with quantities (Ansolabehere et al. 2013). Indeed, the interview data demonstrated that most people conceptualize the political world in relational rather than absolute terms. When explaining issues, almost none of the interview subjects volunteered any specific numbers, even when discussing facts that were fundamentally quantitative in nature. Instead, they would use comparative statements like "China owns most of U.S. debt" or "there isn't enough money being spent on healthcare." For this reason, while asking about specific quantities may yield answers that are useful for researchers, they may not produce answers that accurately reflect how citizens conceptualize political information. Asking about broad concepts and comparisons rather than specific quantities better reflects how most people store and use political knowledge (Olsen 2017). Thus, instead of asking "What percentage of American debt does China own?," I asked participants to assess whether China owns more or less than half of American debt.

Acquiescence bias describes the tendency for survey respondents to agree, both on agree-disagree scales (Pasek and Krosnick 2010) and true-false

Table 2.3 Question wording

Issue area	Correct answer	Incorrect answer
National debt	China holds less than half of U.S. debt.	China holds more than half of U.S. debt.
	Interest on the federal debt is less than half of federal spending.	Interest on the federal debt is more than half of federal spending.
Social welfare	Currently, there is a federal limit on how long a person can receive welfare (TANF) benefits.	Currently, there is no federal limit on how long a person can receive welfare (TANF) benefits.
	Less than 25% of food stamp recipients are children.	More than 25% of food stamp recipients are children.
Government spending	The government spends more on healthcare than on the military.	The government spends more on the military than on healthcare.
	Compared to ten years ago, the percentage of Americans employed by the federal government has decreased.	Compared to ten years ago, the percentage of Americans employed by the federal government has increased.
Immigration	Undocumented immigrants are not eligible to receive food stamps.	Undocumented immigrants are eligible to receive food stamps.
	A child born in the United States to two undocumented immigrants automatically becomes a U.S. citizen.	A child born in the United States to two undocumented immigrants does not automatically become a U.S. citizen.
Entitlement programs	Social Security benefits are paid for by taxes on people who are currently employed.	Social Security benefits are paid for by money that retired people contributed to their Social Security savings account while they were employed.
	Medicare is a federal health insurance program run by the U.S. government for people aged 65 or older.	Medicare is a system of hospitals run by the U.S. government where people 65 or older can get free or reduced-rate medical treatment.
Taxes	A person who makes over $500,000 a year pays more than 25% of their income in taxes.	A person who makes over $500,000 a year pays less than 25% of their income in taxes.
	The largest source of tax revenue in the U.S. is personal income taxes.	The largest source of tax revenue in the U.S. is taxes on corporations.

questions (Schuman and Presser 1996). Offering clear, mutually exclusive response categories presented in random order avoids this issue.

Finally, the follow-up confidence measure can offer some insight into the certainty with which people hold misperceptions. This distinction matters. In a study of factual beliefs about the Affordable Care Act that employed confidence measures, Pasek, Sood, and Krosnick (2015) find that *confidently held* misperceptions are much less common than incorrect answers, which they suggest means that survey questions that ask factual questions without confidence measures may over-estimate the prevalence of false beliefs.[5]

The prevalence of policy misperceptions

On average, participants answered about 6.5 out of the 12 policy questions correctly; slightly better than what we would expect by chance alone. Figure 2.2 displays the distribution of answers for each question graphically. The horizontal axis shows the overall percentage of people who answered incorrectly, including people who were "very confident," "somewhat confident," and "not at all confident" in their answer. The vertical axis shows the average confidence of those who answered incorrectly (on a 0 to 1 scale, with 0 being "not at all confident" and 1 being "very confident"). This measure

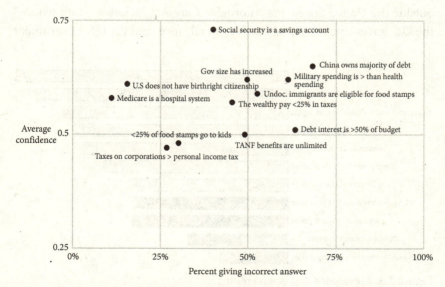

Figure 2.2 Distribution of and confidence in policy misperceptions

helps distinguish between unlucky guesses and firmly entrenched false beliefs. The two questions about entitlement programs illustrate the wide variation in confidence. People who incorrectly believed that Social Security worked liked a savings account were, on average, quite confident in their answer with an average confidence score of .73. In contrast, those who believed that Medicare was a system of hospitals were less certain (.59), suggesting that these incorrect answers may be driven more by ignorance than by misperception.

The most normatively worrisome misperceptions are those in the upper right of Figure 2.2, as they are both widespread and confidently believed: for example, that China owns more than half of U.S. debt and that the U.S. spends more on military than on healthcare. Figure 2.2 also shows that a representative survey can be an important check on misperceptions identified via a qualitative approach: two misperceptions elicited in the interviews—that people born in the United States did not automatically become citizens, and that Medicare was a hospital system—were held by fewer than 20% of respondents.

Figure 2.3 illustrates the reach of the eight misperceptions in that top right-hand quadrant. To put these numbers in context, Figure 2.3 also includes four other false beliefs that have been the subject of media and academic attention, all of which were included as questions on the 2012 American National Election Survey (ANES): that former President Obama was born outside the United States, the Affordable Care Act includes "death panels," the U.S. government knew about 9/11 in advance, and the U.S. government

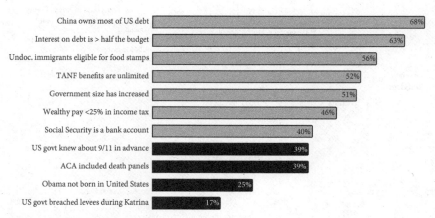

Figure 2.3 Prevalence of misperceptions

* Misperceptions in dark gray are based on 2012 ANES data

was responsible for breaching the levees during Hurricane Katrina in order to preserve middle-class neighborhoods.[6]

As Figure 2.3 shows, many of the policy misperceptions identified in this survey are held by substantially more people than the misperceptions asked about in the ANES. More than two out of three Americans believe that China owns most of U.S. debt and that the interest on the debt is more than half the budget; moreover, around half hold incorrect beliefs about undocumented immigrants, government size, and TANF benefits. In comparison, the most commonly held misperception in the 2012 ANES is the existence of death panels in the Affordable Care Act, which fewer than 40% of Americans believe.

What kinds of people hold misperceptions?

After each factual question, respondents were asked if they were "very," "somewhat," or "not at all" certain that their response was correct. On average, people were confidently wrong on about a third of the questions. In contrast, they were confidently right on about half the questions. Figure 2.4 graphically displays the results of two OLS regressions predicting the total number of confidently held incorrect versus correct beliefs, focusing on factors that past research has been shown to be associated with political knowledge and/or misperceptions.

People who are more educated are less likely to confidently hold incorrect beliefs, and more likely to confidently hold correct beliefs. Intuitively, this is unsurprising since education is highly correlated with political knowledge (Delli Carpini and Keeter 1996; Jennings 1996). However, these results do stand in contrast to some past research showing that people who are more educated are *more* likely to hold political misperceptions. Flynn, Nyhan, and Reifler (2017) point to a potential mechanism for this effect, arguing that those who are highly educated are also more likely to hold stronger and more ideologically consistent views, and thus are more likely to use their partisanship as a (misleading) shortcut when answering highly politicized factual questions. Thus, along with the lack of association with strength of partisanship, these results suggest that the invented state is fundamentally different from the highly politicized misperceptions that are the focus of much existing research.

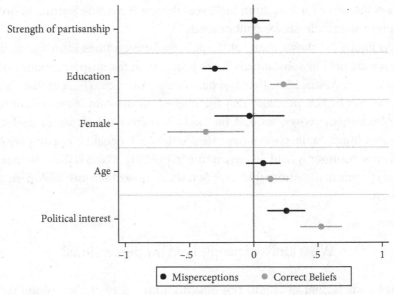

Figure 2.4 Factors associated with confidently holding misperceptions and correct beliefs

The relationship between political interest and factual beliefs is more complicated. People who report following politics more closely hold more correct beliefs, but they also hold more misperceptions. There are several potential explanations for this result. One is that their interest in politics increases the likelihood that they are exposed to misinformation, like "fake news" articles or misleading tweets from politicians. A second explanation, and the argument made in Chapter 4, is that political interest can itself be a trigger for the type of inductive reasoning that creates misperceptions. In other words, people who care about politics are more likely to *think* about politics, and this thinking can lead them to create false beliefs.

Finally, while women tend to score lower than men on surveys assessing political knowledge, some literature suggests that this difference is partly due to the types of questions asked on most political-knowledge batteries (Dolan 2011; Barabas et al. 2014). Figure 2.4 shows that, consistent with past research, women confidently express fewer correct beliefs. It is worth noting, however, that if we set aside the confidence measures and compare only the total number of correct answers, women are equally as accurate as men. This pattern suggests that women do not necessarily know less than men; they are simply less confident in their knowledge. Indeed, women are on the whole substantially less confident (in both their correct and incorrect answers) than men.

The results show no relationship between strength of partisanship and misperceptions. For this set of misperceptions as a whole, there is not the association with strength of partisanship we would expect if they were largely a product of partisan-driven motivated reasoning. This result echoes the pattern observed in the interviews, in which the same misperceptions were invoked by both Democrats and Republicans.

Table 2.4 shows the proportion of Democrats and Republicans who hold each misperception. Many are not sharply divided along partisan lines. Democrats and Republicans are equally likely to believe China holds more than half of U.S. debt, the interest on the debt exceeds 50% of the budget, and Social Security functions as a bank account.

The misperceptions measured in this survey are not entirely unpoliticized. For several, partisans are more likely to hold false beliefs that align with their pre-existing attitudes. Republicans are more likely to say that undocumented immigrants are eligible for food stamps, and Democrats are more likely to think that the rich are taxed at under 25%. This pattern is consistent with past work on factual perceptions and motivated reasoning—people are more likely to answer incorrectly when the fact runs counter to their pre-existing attitudes (Barabas and Jerit 2009).

However, even the policy misperceptions with the widest partisan gaps are still held by large numbers of people in both parties: one in three Republicans think that the richest people in the U.S. pay less than 25% in income tax, and the same number of Democrats believe that government size is increasing.

Table 2.4 Partisans who hold each misperception

	Democrats	Republicans	Total
China owns most of U.S. debt	67%	67%	68%
Interest on debt > half the budget	42%	35%	63%
Undoc. immigrants eligible for food stamps	45%	71%	56%
TANF benefits are unlimited	43%	65%	52%
Government size has increased	37%	71%	51%
Wealthy pay < 25% in income tax	57%	33%	46%
Social Security is a bank account	42%	36%	40%

Conclusion

This chapter investigates the contours of the "invented state": the public's misperceptions about policies. Employing pre-survey interviews makes it possible to identify facts that people spontaneously invoke to explain their opinions. Data from these interviews and a representative survey show that substantial numbers of Americans hold fundamental misperceptions about how government functions. This bottom-up strategy for assessing political knowledge stands in contrast to most previous approaches, which tend to measure either what academics believe people "should" know about politics and policy (Lupia 2006) or the extent to which explicit misinformation (e.g., elite rhetoric or fake news) has altered peoples' political beliefs.

In addition, I outline a specific process for identifying these types of misperceptions. First, I suggest starting with a bottom-up approach; investigating and identifying the types of beliefs (both true and false) that people hold about policies. While the analysis in this chapter begins with interviews, there are a range of other possible approaches to elicit factual beliefs about policy. Open-ended questions in surveys can allow respondents to discuss their beliefs about policy without the bias of interviewer-provided responses. Alternatively, while social media data are often used to better understand opinions (Klašnja et al. 2015), they can also be a rich source of information about factual beliefs. Next, the set of misperceptions identified in this first step can be used to inform a closed-ended survey to measure their prevalence, along with who holds them and the extent to which they are politicized.

The COVID-19 pandemic can illustrate how this process might work in practice. The government response to the pandemic included a number of explicit policies at both the federal and state levels: for example, insurance coverage of vaccines and testing, small business loans, and mask mandates. A study designed to understand misperceptions around these policies might begin with interview or an open-ended survey in which respondents are asked "What sorts of things did the U.S. government do in response to the pandemic?" This initial question could be used to generate a list of salient policies.

Follow-up questions could then probe factual beliefs about the specific policies mentioned most often, and responses could be analyzed to identify commonly held misperceptions. Finally, asking about these misperceptions in a representative closed-ended survey could yield a set of COVID-related policy misperceptions that went well beyond those generated by explicit misinformation.

Perhaps the most striking aspect of the false beliefs identified in this chapter is how different they are from the "fake news" and conspiracy theories that have received so much media and academic attention over the past few years. The misperceptions that make up the invented state are both more widespread and less politicized. To give a specific example, while it is true that nearly a quarter of Americans (almost all Republicans) believe that former President Obama was born outside the United States, nearly three times as many people believe that China owns most of U.S. debt, and the people who hold this misperception are equally likely to be Democrats as Republicans.

Of course, the analyses presented in this chapter are simply a snapshot in time of the invented state as it existed when the data were collected. It is quite possible—and even probable—that these policy misperceptions will shift. Some misperceptions may become politicized: for example, if the national debt becomes a central issue in a presidential election and one candidate explicitly invokes the threat of China, that candidate's supporters may become more likely to believe that China owns the majority of U.S. debt. Other misperceptions may diminish as the issue becomes more central. If Congress debates a new piece of legislation about Social Security, it will likely receive more news coverage, and people will be exposed to more accurate information about how the program works.

However, while change is possible, it is not inevitable. Chapter 7 includes details on a 2018 replication and expansion of the 2014 data analyzed in this chapter. It shows that even across four years, there is remarkable consistency in the distribution of these misperceptions. Still, the larger contribution of this chapter is not the specific misperceptions that I identify. Rather, it offers a proof of concept that this *type* of misperception—false beliefs about existing policy—is widespread.

3
The policy gap in the information environment

During his presidency, Donald Trump repeatedly reduced the U.S. cap on refugees to the lowest numbers since the Refugee Act was passed in 1980. News coverage of Trump's announcements focused heavily on the strategic calculus behind his decision, with the *Washington Post* saying it "reflects the president's increasing vilification of immigrants on the campaign trail" (Miroff 2020). The media also frequently discussed the potential effects of the new cap, with the *New York Times* raising concerns that Trump's actions were "abandoning a moral duty by the United States to be a world leader in the effort to help people in dire situations" (Shear and Kanno-Youngs 2019). Less common in this media coverage were descriptions of the long-standing policies that dictate the practical aspects of U.S. refugee admission and resettlement. Rather than telling readers who qualifies for refugee status and how they enter the United States, coverage instead focused on the political strategy behind the new cap and its potential consequences.

In this chapter, I argue that the media frequently omits basic descriptive information about existing public policy, and that this omission is the product of several systematic biases in news coverage. The first bias is well-documented: the dominance of "strategy frames" that portray politics as a game that can be won or lost (Iyengar et al. 2004). The primacy of strategy coverage means not only that policy is rarely the exclusive focus of news stories but also that when policy *is* covered, it is often through the lens of political tactics. The second bias prioritizes novelty: the media prefer to cover breaking news, not rehash long-standing policies (Bennett 1996b), partly because the public expects and rewards their focus on novelty (Ho and Liu 2015). This tendency results in a systematic bias against coverage of existing policy, especially when that policy is long-standing (e.g., the refugee admission process). The third bias arises because journalists, like all people, suffer from a systematic cognitive bias that psychologists call the "curse of knowledge" (Birch et al. 2017). When someone knows a topic well (e.g., the details of U.S. refugee policy), they tend to assume that others possess the same background knowledge that they do. Indeed, it becomes difficult to imagine *not* knowing this information, making it challenging to communicate about the topic to an audience who knows less (Shatz 2022).

All three of these biases contribute to a media environment in which basic facts about *existing* policies, which I call "policy-current information," appear less frequently in news coverage than does information about *proposed* policies (policy-potential information) or information about the *consequences* of policies (policy-outcome information). In the absence of clear descriptions of existing policy, citizens are left to draw their own conclusions about the status quo—and sometimes those conclusions are wrong.

The first part of this chapter defines policy-current information and discusses why it matters. Then, a content analysis illustrates the relative inclusion of policy-potential, policy-outcome, and policy-current information in news coverage of two issues across three outlets over a decade. The second half of the chapter focuses on how strategy frames, novelty bias, and the curse of knowledge pose particular problems for policy-current coverage.

Policy coverage in the media

This book is far from the first to argue that there is a problem with how the media cover policy. Indeed, journalists themselves are some of the most vocal critics of their (lack of) policy coverage. Writing in the *Washington Post* in 2019, Margaret Sullivan called out the media for "pay[ing] some attention to issues of substance, but mostly as a dutiful side dish—a moderate helping of steamed broccoli that can be shoved to the side of the plate" (Sullivan 2019). Just a few days later, *New York Times* columnist Frank Bruni criticized the media's coverage of Trump during the 2016 election and urged them to focus more on policy in 2020. "Every four years we say we'll devote more energy and space to policy and every four years we don't," he wrote. "But in an environment this polarized and shrill, and at a crossroads this consequential, following through on that vow is more important than ever" (Bruni 2019). Survey data suggest that a substantial portion of the public agrees with Sullivan and Bruni: 38% of people say that the media have failed to provide the "knowledge Americans need to be informed about public affairs" (Gallup

2017). Are Sullivan, Bruni, and 38% of Americans right? The answer to that question depends partly on how we define "policy information."

With good reason, many studies tracking media attention to policy do not distinguish between different types of policy coverage. This approach is especially common in studies of agenda-setting. McCombs and Shaw (1972)'s original study of agenda-setting categorized media coverage into "issue areas" and found a high correlation between the policies that were covered by the media and those that voters said were important. In the decades since, other agenda-setting studies have operationalized policy coverage similarly broadly. For example, in order to measure media attention to climate change, Schmidt, Ivanova, and Schäfer (2013) use a keyword search to find news coverage mentioning (among other terms), climate change, greenhouse effect, and global temperature. Other analyses have tracked the volume of issue coverage by tracking media attention to issues like inflation and welfare (Soroka 2002; Schneider and Jacoby 2005).

For the most part, these analyses do not distinguish between different types of information about policy. For example, in their ambitious cataloguing of the media agenda over time, Atkinson, Lovett, and Baumgartner (2014) examine how often 12 different media outlets cover 90 different issue and policy areas, ranging from NATO to water pollution. Because these broad categories are deliberately agnostic as to what aspects of the issue are covered, they encompass facts, analysis, and/or statements of opinion. For example, stories in the "immigration" category might include an investigation into Texas detention centers, an interview with a candidate about their views on immigration, or a profile of a recent immigrant. While all of these stories are about the *issue* of immigration, not all necessarily reference specific immigration *policy*. To put it another way, not all political coverage discusses issues. Not all issue coverage discusses policies. Not all policy coverage includes factual information. And not all factual information describes currently existing policies.

In this chapter, I distinguish between three types of policy information. The first, policy-outcome information, describes the direct or indirect results of policies (e.g., the percentage of Americans with health insurance and the inflation rate). The second, policy-potential information, describes policies that may be enacted in the future (e.g., proposals from candidates and legislation making its way through Congress). The final category, policy-current information, describes policies that *currently exist*, including relatively recent legislation like the Affordable Care Act (ACA) as well as long-standing

Table 3.1 Examples of policy-potential, policy-outcome, and policy-current information

Issue area	Policy-potential	Policy-outcome	Policy-current
Healthcare	Trump plans to eliminate the individual mandate.	In 2019, 92% of people in the U.S. had health insurance.	The ACA allows parents to add children to their policies until age 26.
Immigration	Pelosi's new proposal includes an earned pathway to citizenship for 11 million undocumented immigrants.	Immigrants today account for 13.7% of the U.S. population.	There is a limit to how many immigrants can come to the U.S. from any one country.
Education	The Democratic-led House appropriations subcommittee that oversees the education budget seeks to cut the federal charter school fund by $40 million.	The average class size in U.S. elementary schools is about 22 students.	To receive federal school funding, states must give assessments in basic skills.

policies like Social Security. Table 3.1 provides examples of the three types of policy information for three issue areas: healthcare, immigration, and education.

Policy-potential information

Policy-potential information describes policies that have the *potential* to become enacted, including bills under debate in Congress and candidates' policy proposals. The question of whether the media provides sufficient policy-potential coverage is especially relevant during elections. When people are choosing between candidates for office, those candidates' policy stances are (or at least, should be) an important part of voters' decision-making. Thus, a number of studies have examined the extent to which campaign coverage includes information about the candidates' policy positions. For example, Patterson (2016) codes media coverage of the 2016 election into four major categories: horse race, controversies, "other," and "policy stances." This last category includes coverage of policy proposals like Hillary Clinton's paid family leave policy and Trump's commitment to building a wall between the U.S. and Mexico. In 2016, policy stances made up only 10% of the total coverage of the campaign. This pattern is not unique to that election: for the last 50 years, horse race coverage has been consistently increasing, and coverage of the candidates' policy stances decreasing (Benoit et al. 2005; Sigelman and Bullock 1991; Andersen and Thorson 1989).

While policy-potential information is clearly important, people may struggle to understand candidates' proposed policy changes without a baseline understanding of *existing* policy. For example, during a 2009 South Carolina town hall held to discuss the Affordable Care Act, an attendee famously told Rep. Rob Inglis (R-SC) to "keep your government hands off my Medicare," not realizing that Medicare is a government-run program (Rucker 2009). Understanding *existing* policy is thus critical for evaluating *potential* policies.

Policy-outcome information

Information in the policy-outcome category concerns the direct or indirect *outcomes* of policies, often expressed as quantities or rates. For example, policy-outcome information related to immigration includes the number of immigrants who entered the country in the last year, the proportion of deportations handled by state police versus ICE (Immigration and Custom Enforcement), and the average waiting time for immigration court. Policy-outcome information about the Affordable Care Act (ACA) includes the percent of Americans who are uninsured, the average cost of prescription drugs, or the number of people covered via the Medicaid expansion. All of this information speaks to *outcomes* of immigration policy and the ACA rather than describing what the policies actually entail.

The connection between outcomes, particularly performance indicators like the unemployment rate, and policies is often murky, and thus their interpretation can be especially susceptible to partisan-driven motivated reasoning. Even if people accept that a particular outcome (e.g., a drop in unemployment) is true, they often rationalize that outcome in a way that confirms their pre-existing beliefs, including by shifting where they assign responsibility. Bisgaard (2019) illustrates this tendency in a series of experiments in which participants are provided with either positive or negative facts about economic performance. While subjects update their factual beliefs in accordance with the new information, they *interpret* those beliefs differently depending on their partisanship, blaming opponents for bad news and giving credit to co-partisans for good news. In other words, "although citizens with strong partisan loyalties may accept the same facts, they find alternative ways to rationalize reality" (Bisgaard 2019, 825). Chapter 5 discusses how partisanship shapes factual interpretation in more detail.

Policy-current information

Policy-current information describes policies currently in place, including both those that have been in place for generations (e.g., aspects of Social Security) and those that are more recent (e.g., the Affordable Care Act). Examples of policy-current information includes who is eligible for particular social welfare programs, tax brackets, and employment regulations.

Of course, as with any classificatory system, not all pieces of information fall neatly into a single category. For example, the survey described in Chapter 1 finds that more than three in five people mistakenly believe that China owns the majority of U.S. debt. This misperception occupies a gray zone between "policy-current" and "policy-outcome." While the percentage of debt owned by China is not dictated by a specific policy, it is also not clearly the outcome of a policy. Throughout the book, I tend to classify facts like these as policy-current if the quantity in question has remained relatively stable for a long period of time. In this case, China has *always* owned substantially less than half of U.S. debt.

Why policy-current information matters

It is easy to see why knowledge of a candidate's policy proposals is important: we expect that people will choose candidates based partly on what policies they promise to enact. Similarly, performance facts matter because they serve as the basis for retrospective voting as well as thermostatic responsiveness more generally (Page and Shapiro 2010; Wlezien 1995; Soroka and Wlezien 2022). In this section, I argue that policy-current information is also important for democratic functioning. First, it helps people draw connections between policies and outcomes, which can improve accountability. Second, understanding existing policy makes it possible to better evaluate proposals for how to change it.

A baseline level of knowledge about existing policies makes it easier to integrate new information. As an example, consider the policy-outcome fact that the rate of Americans who are uninsured decreased between 2014 and 2016. This drop occurred largely because of the Affordable Care Act, which imposed a penalty for not having health insurance, established health insurance exchanges, and expanded Medicaid. Understanding what the ACA actually did makes it possible to draw a connection between the bill's passage and the drop in the uninsured rate.[1]

Policy-current information also helps people evaluate policy proposals. For example, learning that Joe Biden wants to reinstate Deferred Action for Childhood Arrivals (DACA) is meaningless without knowing what DACA is. But this principle also extends to more familiar policies like Medicare. During the 2020 election, Biden made headlines with his proposal to lower the Medicare eligibility age to 60. But evaluating this proposal requires background knowledge, including the current eligibility age and what benefits Medicare confers.

What types of policy facts do the media include?

To what extent do the media include policy-current, policy-outcome, and policy-potential information in their issue coverage? Most media content analyses measure the presence or absence of policy coverage rather than the *type* of policy information included. This section presents the results of a descriptive content analysis designed to answer this question across two separate policy issues.

Content analysis design

I focus on media coverage of two issues: Medicare and immigration. Both issues are a perennial aspect of the political landscape. As of 2018, about 18% of Americans were enrolled in the Medicare program, including 90% of adults over age 50 (Mercado 2018), and Medicare figured heavily in debates over the Affordable Care Act. Immigration has also been a focal point of politics over the last decade, with Donald Trump emphasizing the issue during his 2016 campaign (Corasaniti 2016).

The content analysis includes articles from three outlets: *USA Today*, the *New York Times*, and the Associated Press. The first two outlets are some of the highest-circulating newspapers in the country. The Associated Press provides content to over 1,700 news outlets, including hundreds of local papers in the United States. Articles were taken from a 10-year time period (2009–2019), which includes two presidential elections and four midterm elections. To construct the universe of eligible articles, I conducted a search on LexisUni for any article in the three publications that included "Medicare" in the headline published in this timeframe (in total, 1,165 articles). For immigration, I included all articles with "immigration" in the headline and the word "policy" in the headline or lead paragraph (in total, 1,464 articles).

It is important to note that the design of this study is deliberately biased toward identifying articles that include policy information. Medicare is itself a policy, and restricting the immigration articles to those that include the word "policy" in the headline or lead drastically reduces the universe of immigration-related articles. For example, in 2018 the *New York Times* published 223 articles with "immigration" in the headline, but only 66 of those headlines included the word "policy" in the headline or lead paragraph. Limiting the universe to policy-focused articles is a deliberate choice because the goal of this content analysis is to answer the question "what types of factual information are included in policy coverage?" rather than "how often do the media cover policy?" While the latter question is an important one, it is beyond the scope of this chapter.

From each set of articles, I randomly selected 200 to be coded for the inclusion of policy facts. Two research assistants were given a codebook defining policy-potential, policy-current, and policy-outcome facts, including extensive examples and illustrations. After practicing on a training set of articles, they were instructed to count the total number of policy-potential, policy-current, and policy-outcome facts in each article. They were asked to exclude any articles that were either under 200 words (most often, letters to the editor) or that were exclusively about another country (e.g., an article about European immigration).

Results

The substantial majority of articles (94%) included at least one of the three types of policy facts, with the median article including four. As Table 3.2

44 THE INVENTED STATE

Table 3.2 Inclusion of policy information in Medicare and immigration coverage

	Total		Immigration		Medicare	
	Average	None	Average	None	Average	None
Policy-current	1.9	41%	1.7	55%	2.1	45%
Policy-potential	2.8	33%	2.5	51%	3.1	49%
Policy-outcome	2.1	35%	1.9	56%	2.2	44%

Note: Average refers to the average number of policy facts of each type included per article. "None" refers to the proportion of articles that included in which each type of fact was entirely absent.

shows, policy-current information was least common. The average article included 1.9 policy-current facts, but fully 41% of articles included no descriptive factual information about existing policies. This number is especially surprising given that these articles were deliberately selected for their focus on policy.

About a third of the articles included no facts about policy-potential, and a third included no facts about policy-outcomes. These patterns are similar across the two issues, suggesting that the dearth of policy-current information may be a result of larger journalistic norms rather than an idiosyncrasy of one particular topic.

Figure 3.1 presents the results of a regression analysis predicting the number of policy-current facts included. It includes the issue topic (reference category is immigration), section (reference category is news), outlet (reference category is the Associated Press), inclusion of the other two types of policy information, the word count, and whether the article was written in the six months prior to a federal election.

Articles appearing in the opinion section are significantly less likely to include policy-current information. There is also a negative association between policy-current facts and policy-potential facts: the more information an article includes about proposed policies, the less information it has about existing policies. Although Figure 3.1 should not be interpreted as evidence of causal relationships between the variables, the negative association between policy-potential and policy-current information is normatively concerning nonetheless. It may be difficult for people to evaluate new policies if they are not provided with information about existing policy. For example, a 2012 *New York Times* article headlined "Obama and Ryan Trade Blasts Over

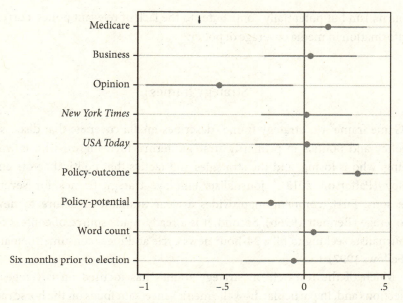

Figure 3.1 Factors associated with the inclusion of policy-current information

Medicare at AARP Convention" described both politicians' doomsaying about their opponents' plans and contained two policy-potential facts and no policy-current facts (Landler and Oppel 2012). The article described Obama's claims that Republican proposals might turn Medicare into a voucher program that could raise the cost of care for many older people, and Ryan's counter that entitlement reform has been made overly partisan. However, the article was silent on how a "voucher program" differed from the current Medicare policy or what an entitlement actually is. Given this lack of context, a reader might be understandably confused about how to evaluate these two competing proposals.

Systematic barriers to policy-current coverage

This section discusses three major factors that contribute to the lack of policy-current coverage in the media. The first two, strategy frames and novelty bias, are well-documented sources of distortion, and I argue that they are particularly powerful in shaping minimizing policy-current coverage. The third factor, the so-called curse of knowledge, is less discussed in the context of journalism but potentially contributes to the lack of relevant policy-current information in media coverage of policy.

Strategy frames

"Game frame" or "strategy frame" describes media coverage that discusses policy and politics in primarily strategic terms, focusing on who is winning, who is losing, and the strategies and tactics that political actors employ (Patterson 2013).[2] Journalists employ strategy frames for several reasons. First, competition provides a clear dramatic structure to news coverage (Bennett 1996b). Second, it is a ready-made source of content for journalists seeking to fill a 24-hour news cycle and meet consumer demand (Fallows 1997).

Much of the research on strategy frames has focused on coverage of elections and, in particular, how the media's incessant focus on the horse race can crowd out coverage of the candidate's policy positions (Patterson 2011). Journalists also use strategy frames in a non-electoral context, in particular when policymakers are "engaged in legislative 'conflict with movement' that promises a clear outcome (i.e., the passage or rejection of legislation) on issues that are highly consequential politically" (Lawrence 2000, 98).

The media's preference for strategy frames means that policies receive especially heavy coverage *before* they are enacted, as Congress debates and negotiates what is and is not included. The media's tendency to focus on these policy debates is normatively desirable, as a transparent legislative process provides opportunities for the public to influence eventual outcomes. However, coverage of the policymaking process is heavily tilted toward "descriptions of partisan combat" rather than substantive information (Atkinson 2017).

While the flurry of coverage that occurs during a policy's passage is important, it is insufficient to keep the public informed, especially given the longevity of many policies. Only around 20% of all federal law has been repealed or nullified by Congress (Whyman 2018), which means that most Americans were simply not alive to read the media coverage surrounding most policies' inceptions. Millions of voters in the 2020 presidential election were in middle school when the Affordable Care act was debated. Medicare was passed in 1965: before three-quarters of 2020 electorate was even born.

The vast majority of people did not get to experience the debates and discussion surrounding the genesis of most public policy.

Even after a policy is enacted, journalists are drawn to the political aspects of its implementation. Gollust et al. (2017) examined 3,000 local news stories about the Affordable Care Act broadcast during the seven-month open enrollment period in 2013–2014. They classified each story as being mainly about the politics of the ACA, the actual products available and the enrollment process, or a combination of both. In addition to the story topic, they also coded for the inclusion of individual facts, including both policy-current facts (details about coverage and how to enroll) and policy-outcome facts (number of enrollees, problems with the ACA website).

Over half the stories included at least some coverage of the politics of the ACA, but policy-current information was less common. Only 7% mentioned Medicaid or the Medicaid expansion, despite the importance of this program to the ACA. In contrast, a third of the stories mentioned website glitches experienced by HealthCare.gov, often in the context of what they meant for the political success of the program. Overall, they concluded that the news discussed the law "using a political strategy frame (similar to political campaign coverage), thus limiting citizens' exposure to the substance of ACA policy content while heightening the public's likelihood of perceiving the law via politically charged heuristics" (Gollust et al. 2017, 691).

The media's reliance on the game frame reduces policy-current coverage through two channels. First, it reduces coverage of *all* policy issues in favor of horse race and strategy coverage Second, even when the media do cover policy, they may be less likely to include descriptions of existing policy since that information is less relevant to the "game" of politics.

Novelty bias

One of the primary duties of the media is to report the news: to quite literally tell the public about what is *new*. Journalists are trained to see timeliness as a professional duty (Deuze 2005), and the public expects it as well: novelty increases news readership (Ho and Liu 2015). The media's relentless focus on novelty has two separate but related effects on how they cover policy. First, media coverage of policy often focuses on *change* and ignores the many aspects that remain the same year after year. Second, policies that are static rarely receive coverage at all.

There are many good normative reasons for the media to emphasize change over stasis. Insofar as the media's job is to alert the public to problems and debates in politics, covering long-standing policy might seem unnecessary and even confusing (Zaller 2003). And indeed, by some measures the media area successful at both sounding "burglar alarms" about policy failures and keeping the public apprised of macro-shifts in policy outcomes. Soroka and Wlezien (2022) find that the media are surprisingly effective at communicating changes in government spending in specific issue areas. Information about changes in spending is undeniably important: the public deserves to know how its money is being spent. However, a baseline understanding of existing policy provides important context for evaluating spending changes. In addition, not all policies can be easily summarized via spending. For example, healthcare spending is a poor barometer of whether people are actually receiving quality care.

When policies do change, media coverage often focuses on that change at the expense of other relevant background information. An illustrative example is the Medicaid expansion that happened as part of the Affordable Care Act. The fundamental aim of the Medicaid program—to ensure low-income Americans have access to health coverage—has remained the same since it was established in 1965. Because Medicaid is administered at the state level, there is variation between states in who is eligible. The Affordable Care Act, passed in 2010, expanded the eligibility threshold to allow more people to participate in the program. However, a Supreme Court decision in June 2012 effectively made it optional for states to participate in the expansion.

The consequent decisions by states about whether to participate in the program were novel, and as such received substantial media coverage. Several state courts also heard challenges related to Medicaid expansion. For example, a December 2018 article in the *Idaho Spokesman-Review* describing a state Supreme Court challenge to Medicaid expansion provides a number of details about the legal challenge, including who was leading it, how it was funded, the schedule for the court hearings, and the status of similar challenges in other states (Talericao 2018). However, the article includes no details about the Medicaid program itself other than the single phrase "coverage of low-income and childless adults." It does not mention how many Idahoans are covered by Medicaid, the income threshold for coverage, or that the expansion was related to the Affordable Care Act. In other words, while the article does an admirable job of explaining what is *new* about Medicaid (in this case, the legal challenge), it provides almost no information about the existing Medicaid program.

Finally, this focus on novelty necessarily excludes a number of long-standing policies. Many of the country's largest policies (both in terms of spending and number of people affected) have been in place for generations. As Mettler (2011) points out, many of the largest social tax expenditures are over a century old. The home mortgage tax deduction was enacted in 1913, and the deductibility of charitable contributions was established in 1917. Farm subsidies were enacted after the Great Depression, and the current preference system for immigrants was a part of the 1965 Hart-Celler Act.

The prioritization of novelty over context can lead to what Bennett calls "fragmentation," in which "stories suffer from the absence of meaningful connection to each other . . . [and] long-term trends and historical patterns are seldom made a part of the news" (Bennett 1996b, 19). On a practical level, this means that even when the media *does* cover policy, that coverage tends to focus (1) on novel rather than long-standing policy and (2) on the dynamic rather than static aspects of a given policy.

The curse of knowledge

The "curse of knowledge" describes how people's own knowledge of an issue or topic can alter their beliefs about what *others* know: "The tendency to be biased by one's own current knowledge state when trying to appreciate a more naive perspective" (Birch and Bloom 2007, 382). The term was first coined by economists, who used the concept to explain a puzzle. In theory, having information that a competitor does not have should provide a competitive advantage. But across multiple experiments, actors who had that additional information did not take full advantage of it. Instead, they acted as if others also knew it, thus unintentionally minimizing their informational advantage. In other words, they tended to "overestimate the knowledge of less-informed agents" (Camerer et al. 1989, 1245).[3]

Or consider the game of charades. A person acting out the character of "Sherlock Holmes" by making a magnifying glass out of their fingers may find it absolutely incomprehensible that the people on their team mistake the magnifying glass for a monocle and insist on guessing "Mr. Peanut." The curse of knowledge can make it difficult for people who know a topic well to communicate about it to novices. As Stephen Pinker put it in a 2014 *Wall Street Journal* article:

> The curse of knowledge is the single best explanation of why good people write bad prose. It simply doesn't occur to the writer that her readers don't know what she knows—that they haven't mastered the argot of her guild, can't divine the missing steps that seem too obvious to mention, have no way to visualize a scene that to her is as clear as day. And so the writer doesn't bother to explain the jargon, or spell out the logic, or supply the necessary detail. (Pinker 2014)

The problems created by the curse of knowledge have been studied extensively in the area of science communication, where research has focused on helping scientists communicate their findings effectively to citizens and avoid jargon (Sharon and Baram-Tsabari 2014). However, journalism does not have parallel guidance, and as such there is little practical advice on how to distill complex policy topics in a way that people can understand.

The organizational structure of media outlets exacerbates the curse of knowledge. Many journalists are assigned to "beats," which allows them to cover the same topic for months, if not years (Bennett 1996a). For example, a reporter might focus largely on healthcare policy or the Supreme Court. This division of responsibility is efficient, allowing the reporter to build networks of sources, ask pertinent questions, and gain a nuanced understanding of the issue. However, journalists' deep expertise can also subtly hinder their ability to write articles that people *without* that same contextual knowledge can comprehend. Indeed, when editors were asked to estimate the grade level at which news stories were written, they consistently overestimated their readability—on average, by 4.2 grade levels (Porter and Stephens 1989). Other research has similarly demonstrated that a substantial amount of news content is written in a way that is difficult for a novice audience to understand and that hard news is among the most complex (Wasike 2018).

Case study: Media coverage of the national debt in 2014

In the following section, I analyze coverage of the national debt in 2014 to illustrate how strategy frames, novelty bias, and the curse of knowledge shape the inclusion (or lack thereof) of policy-current information. I focus on the national debt for two reasons. First, two of the most commonly held misperceptions identified in Chapter 2 directly concerned the debt. More than two-thirds of Americans incorrectly believe that China owns most of U.S. debt and that the interest on the national debt is more than half the federal budget. In reality, China owns around 8% of U.S. debt, and interest on the debt is about 7% of the national budget. Second, in 2014 (also the year the survey in Chapter 2 was fielded), the national debt received a substantial amount of media coverage (explained below) and so is illustrative of how the media covers a particularly salient policy issue.

In early 2013, the U.S. entered a crisis when Republican members of Congress refused to raise the debt ceiling unless then-President Obama agreed to defund parts of the Affordable Care Act. The crisis was finally resolved in October, when the Senate agreed to both fund the government and suspend the debt ceiling until early 2014. In February of 2014, the debt limit suspension expired, and Republicans once again tested the water on resisting an increase. However, met with public skepticism, they capitulated by mid-February and the debt ceiling was once again extended.

The national debt was also an issue during the 2014 congressional campaigns, with candidates on both sides criticizing how members of the other party dealt with the debt. Perhaps because of the 2013 crisis, public concern over the national debt was at a relative high in 2014. In January of that year, 52% of Americans said that their level of concern over the issue had increased a lot over the last few years. Five years later, that number dropped to 40% (Peter G. Peterson Foundation 2019). Overall, in 2014 the national debt was an important issue both to politicians and to the public.

Coding news coverage of the national debt

The content analysis was designed to answer two questions: First, to what extent does media coverage of the national debt include relevant contextual information? Second, to what extent might the biases outlined above shape the factual information that is included in (or absent from) the coverage? The articles and transcripts to be analyzed were identified via a search on LexisUni for the keywords "national debt" or "federal debt" or "U.S. debt" appearing in television transcripts from CBS, CNN, FOX, and MSNBC and news articles from the *Washington Post, New York Times, USA Today*, and the Associated Press between January 1 and December 31, 2014.

Articles and transcripts that did not explicitly mention the national debt in the United States (e.g., a *New York Times* article headlined "Italy Gasps as Inquiry Reveals Mob's Long Reach" discussed Italy's national debt rather than that of the U.S.) were eliminated. The final data set included 298 total stories: 147 television transcripts and 151 news articles. Each piece was coded for whether it included each of the following four pieces of policy-relevant information:

- The national debt has increased (policy-outcome).
- The amount (absolute or relative) of the national debt (policy-current).
- To whom the national debt is owed (policy-current).
- The amount (absolute or relative) of interest on the national debt (policy-current).

In addition, the pieces were coded for whether they included statements about the consequences or effects of the national debt (policy-outcome), and if so, what those consequences would be.

This coding scheme was designed to be a fairly easy test for whether news coverage of the national debt includes relevant information. Coders were not required to check whether the number or facts were accurate or whether they included partial or complete information—only if the pieces of information were present in the article.

Few facts in coverage of the national debt

Table 3.3 shows that only 36% of stories mentioning the national debt provided *any* of the four pieces of information. The fact most likely to be included was the total amount of debt, which was mentioned in 23% of the articles. Print and broadcast journalism were equally (un)likely to include factual information: 33% of broadcast transcripts and 38% of print articles included one of the facts.

One critical question, then, is exactly what *was* included, if not factual information? A closer look at the 64% of articles that included none of these facts gives a sense of how the national debt was discussed in media coverage. In the following section, I draw on examples to illustrate how strategy frames and novelty bias both shape what factual information is and is not included in media coverage of the national debt.

Table 3.3 Inclusion of factual information in 2014 national debt coverage

	Percent of articles
Amount of debt	23%
Debt has increased	16%
Amount of interest	7%
To whom debt is owed	5%
Any of the above	**36%**

Strategy coverage

Strategy coverage of the national debt took two major forms. In the first, the national debt was invoked as part of campaign rhetoric, often as part of a quote from a politician. In the second, it was characterized as a political bargaining chip.

When the national debt was part of a candidate's rhetoric, journalists rarely provided additional context to help readers interpret the remarks. For example, a February *New York Times* article broke the news that Lieutenant Governor John Walsh had been appointed to fill a vacant Senate seat left in Montana. The article mentioned Walsh's plans to "focus on reducing spending and the national debt," but it did not provide any details about that plan or the debt itself (Healy 2014). In April, Fox's Greta Van Susterern hosted California Republican congressional candidate Carl Demaio (Van Susteren 2014). Demaio mentioned the national debt twice during his brief appearance on the show, first demanding that Washington refocus its priorities on "fixing the national debt" and then that the government be "held accountable" for the national debt. Demaio included no additional information about the debt, and Van Susterern did not question him on the issue.

In other stories, the national debt was invoked as a bargaining chip. A CNN story describing the legacy of the Tea Party movement described how it brought national attention to the debt: "The Tea Party changed the conversation through its laser focus on issues such as the national debt, the federal budget and entitlement spending ... The refusal by Tea Party Republicans in the House to accept business-as-usual compromises on federal spending caused a series of showdowns with Obama and Democrats." The article goes on to discuss the strategies the Tea Party used to reduce spending and lower the debt, including sequestration, but provides no factual information about the debt itself (Cohen 2014).

In both types of coverage, the national debt is portrayed as a piece on the political chessboard, either as an aspect of campaign rhetoric, or as a part of the strategic maneuvering between political elites. There is little context as to why the debt matters, how it affects Americans, or what it actually is.

Novelty bias
When substantive coverage of the debt was included, it was often through the lens of what was new. A *New York Times* article entitled "A Dire Economic Forecast Based on New Assumptions" illustrates this tendency. The story reported on new economic forecasts from the Congressional Budget Office, characterizing them as a "dreary, depressing prospect" and predicting that interest rates on the national debt would rise (Norris 2014). However, despite the national debt being a major focus of the article, there was no information about the amount of debt, to whom it was owed, or the current interest payments. Only the potential change was discussed.

Similarly, a piece from the Associated Press discussed the national debt in the context of the GOP's April budget proposal. In particular, they mentioned Paul Ryan's plan to cut several programs in order to "get serious about the national debt." However, no details about the debt are included. Overall, in discussing the national debt, news coverage tended to focus on what is new (whether a new budget plan or new projections) and omitted basic background information.

Conclusion

Both politicians and the media that cover them thus have an enormous incentive to talk about politics rather than policy. These incentives have helped create a world in which politicians frequently invoke the national debt but rarely mention to whom that debt is owed, and where newspapers run stories about Social Security's solvency without explaining how the program is funded. Media coverage focuses on policy changes rather than providing the background information arguable necessary for understanding and contextualizing those changes. Americans—even those who consume news regularly—thus lack consistent access to the background information they need to understand public policy.

To what extent might social media fill in this blank? Unfortunately, the prospect of social media as a fount of policy information seems unlikely. Most people consume relatively little news on social media in the first place (Allen et al. 2020), and to the extent that issue coverage does appear on social media, it tends to follow the same general parameters as elite discourse (Gilardi et al. 2022). In addition, the news that is *shared* on social media may be even less likely to include accurate policy information (Soroka and Wlezien 2022).

Media coverage of a policy can contribute to the creation of misperceptions even without explicitly disseminating misinformation. When a news story provides only fragmented information, it can lead people to make incorrect inferences. Jerit and Barabas (2006) show how misleading rhetoric about Social Security contributed to incorrect inferences about the future of the program. They pair a content analysis of media coverage of the 1998–1999 debate over Social Security with survey data from the same period, and they find that when media coverage of Social Security included more misleading elite rhetoric (statements like "Social Security will begin to go bankrupt if we don't find solutions now"), people were more likely to incorrectly state that the program would run out of money completely if no reforms were made. This effect was heightened among those who reported following the issue closely.

In this chapter, I argue that the lack of systematic coverage of existing policy has real consequences for public knowledge. This omission creates a vacuum that allows—and in some cases, even encourages—citizens to make their own (often incorrect) factual inferences about government policy. This is a more complicated argument than simply "the media misinforms people." Of course it is possible for the media to actively disseminate misinformation, either deliberately (an entrepreneur writing an eye-catching "fake news" story to generate advertising revenue) or inadvertently (a reporter repeats a statistic that turns out to be incorrect). But explicit misinformation is not the only way that media coverage contributes to misperceptions. False beliefs can emerge when people "fill in the blank" with their own assumptions about politics and policies through a process of inductive reasoning. Chapter 4 details this process of inductive reasoning and offers evidence of how it can generate misperceptions.

4
The construction of beliefs about policy

When my daughter was three years old, she became fascinated with firefighting. During a car ride, she demanded to know exactly how the firefighters got water from fire hydrants, and I answered her with as much detail as I could muster. Although my description included a number of facts, I did not pull these facts from a mental library of fire hydrant mechanics. Rather, I actively *constructed* much of the information I relayed to her, drawing on half-remembered trips to the fire station when I was a child, my understanding of physics, and common sense. Some of the factual inferences I made turned out to be correct (the water that comes out of fire hydrants is indeed the same water that we drink). Others did not (firefighters do not open the hydrants with a special key—instead, they use a pentagonal wrench).

As I explained to my daughter how fire hydrants worked, I was actively engaging in inductive reasoning, or what psychologists call "everyday reasoning" (Feeney and Heit 2007). Inductive reasoning, or "using existing knowledge to make predictions about novel cases," is fundamental to how we navigate the world (Hayes and Heit 2018, 1).[1] We engage in inductive reasoning when we glance out the window to predict the day's weather or decide to wear a mask to work because COVID rates are surging. Sherlock Holmes, the ultimate inductive reasoner, could from a single glance infer someone's occupation, mental state, and criminal background. While most of us will never reach Holmes's level of acuity, we all possess a similar set of skills that allow us to draw factual inferences about novel objects, people, and—critically for this book—policies.

This book is about how and why people come to hold misperceptions about policy. While reading "fake news" is one route to becoming misinformed, there is another way that people come to hold false beliefs: they create them themselves. In this chapter, I argue that when we decide that an issue has personal relevance to us, we spend more time and energy thinking about that issue. And in the process of thinking about it, we not only generate opinions ("the national debt is bad") but also factual inferences ("the national debt is increasing"). Some of these facts come from memory: we recall what we have read or seen or heard about the topic. But others are products of inductive reasoning: we draw on related knowledge to make assumptions—sometimes misguided ones—about what is or could be true. Simply *thinking* about policies contributes what we know—and get wrong—about how the government actually works.

Inductive reasoning and policy misperceptions

Many factual beliefs (either correct or incorrect) about policy are a direct result of learning (Gilens 2001). People learn about policy from the media, from formal education, from their social networks, and from personal experience. But learning is not the only source of political beliefs. As Chapter 3 explains, the media's focus on novelty and tendency toward strategic political coverage means that facts about existing policy (e.g., the basics of how Social Security works) receive relatively little coverage, making it more difficult for the public to learn this information. Inductive reasoning is one way that people fill these gaps.

Walter Lippmann's account of how individuals create their own political realities is partly a story of inductive reasoning. In the first half of *Public Opinion*, he explains how citizens' factual beliefs are informed by both external information and pre-existing beliefs: "This trickle of messages from the outside is affected by the stored up images, the preconceptions, and prejudices which interpret, fill them out, and in their turn powerfully direct the play of our attention, and our vision itself" (Lippmann 1922, 30).

Most of us have likely observed inductive reasoning in the political realm firsthand. Over the course of one particular family dinner argument, my aunt generated many facts about election law (few of which bore much resemblance to actual statutes). And while her inferences may have missed the mark, it is important to note that inductive reasoning can also produce accurate knowledge—indeed, the development of inductive reasoning skills is a critical part of the learning process (Koning et al. 2002). Inductive reasoning can help us draw useful and valid inferences about policy. But it also has the potential to lead us astray, creating misperceptions.

This chapter tries to answer two fundamental questions about how inductive reasoning creates policy misperceptions. The first asks why people engage in inductive reasoning around some policies but not others. In a world where attention is limited and political interest is often minimal, under what circumstances do people bother engaging in the cognitive work of making inferences about a particular policy? I answer this question with an experiment, showing how personal relevance can spur inductive reasoning.

The second question is descriptive: When we engage in inductive reasoning, what kinds of explanations do we invent, and why are they sometimes incorrect? I draw on the responses to open-ended survey questions to explore how specific strategies of inductive reasoning might lead people astray. Finally, I conclude by highlighting the importance of these findings for our understanding of what citizens know—and get wrong—about policy.

What catalyzes inductive reasoning?

Whether we are walking down the street, browsing Facebook, or looking at a restaurant menu, it is impossible for us to devote equal cognitive attention to every person, post, and entree. Similarly, when it comes to politics, our attention is limited. We only have the time and energy to think about a small fraction of the enormous universe of political issues. This section is concerned with answering the question of why we engage in inductive reasoning about some policies but not others. Identifying the catalysts for inductive reasoning makes it possible to predict when people will form misperceptions as opposed to simply remaining ignorant. This distinction matters because a citizen who is uninformed behaves differently than one who is misinformed (Kuklinski et al. 2000; Pasek, Sood, et al. 2015).

In general, people engage in inductive reasoning when they perceive that it can help them to achieve their goals (Sloman and Fernbach 2018). For example, if I encounter a large spider in my kitchen, I will likely make a quick inference about the spider (in particular, its likelihood of biting me) as I decide whether to crush it or gently carry it outside (Krawczyk 2017). In this case, I engage in inductive reasoning because it is immediately useful for me to do so.

We can also think of engaging in inductive reasoning as a type of information-seeking. Most information-seeking involves external sources, like newspapers, friends, or Facebook. Inductive reasoning is the process of seeking out information *internally*, by drawing on existing knowledge and logical inference. Because both information-seeking and inductive reasoning have the same ultimate goal of increasing knowledge, the theories that scholars have developed to understand when and why people seek out external information may also shed light on why people engage in inductive reasoning.

Studies of information-seeking try to understand why people choose to seek out and consume one piece of content rather than another. While a long literature examines the choice between news and entertainment (Prior 2007, 2018; Ruggiero 2000), I am specifically interested here in how people decide to seek out information about particular political topics. For example, why does one person choose to read an article about healthcare while another opts for a piece about the stock market?

The theory of "informational utility" argues that a person is more likely to read a particular news story if it helps them "adapt to and cope with the environment" (Knobloch-Westerwick 2014, 159). In the political context, this means a person will be more likely to consume information about an issue if they perceive that it will affect them personally, especially if the effects are highly likely and will occur sooner rather than later (Knobloch-Westerwick et al. 2005; Carpentier 2008). To test the informational utility model experimentally, Knobloch, Carpentier, and Zillmann (2003) present subjects with a fabricated online newspaper. The newspaper includes a range of headlines, some of which have been manipulated to be either more or less likely to affect the reader. For example, the low-likelihood headline of an article about meningitis read "Meningitis Losing to Education and Vaccination, Cases Declining," while the high-likelihood version read "Meningitis Shocks CDC with Ever-Increasing Evidence of Contagion." Across two experiments and three different issues, the results were consistent: people were more likely to click on and spend more time reading headlines that affected them than those that did not.

When it comes to selecting news, topic relevance is even more important than the partisanship of the news source (e.g., Fox News vs MSNBC) in determining whether someone chooses to read a particular story (Mummolo 2016). For example, seniors are significantly more likely than non-seniors to select a story headlined "Congress Weighs Cuts to Social Security," regardless of whether it comes from a news source aligned with their partisanship.

If inductive reasoning is indeed spurred by the same factors that shape information-seeking, then people will be more likely to make factual inferences about policies that are personally relevant. Nadeau and Niemi (1995) test this hypothesis with cross-sectional survey data. Their results show that when people perceive an issue to be more important, they are less likely to answer "don't know" to factual questions about that issue. For example, people who believe debates about the French language in Quebec are relevant are less likely to respond "don't know" when asked to estimate the percentage of Francophones in Quebec. Niemi and Nadeau argue that this relationship exists because people who care more about an issue are more likely to "use cues in answering factual questions just as they use top-of-head considerations in responding to queries about issues" (Nadeau and Niemi 1995, 340). In other words, they are more likely to engage in inductive reasoning.

> Anyone who has played question-and-answer games such as Trivial Pursuit knows that there is more to answering factual information questions than simply knowing the answer or not knowing it. Sometimes one can figure out what the answer "must be"—by a process of elimination, by reasoning from known, related facts, by various methods of approximation, and so on. (Nadeau and Niemi 1995, 340)

However, their evidence is not conclusive proof of a causal relationship, because personal relevance may also lead people to seek out (or at least pay attention to) external information about that issue. Thus, there is an equally plausible explanation for this observed relationship: that people who care about the debate over the French language in Quebec are more likely to read about the issue, talk to friends about the issue, and otherwise become informed (or misinformed)—as well as more likely to recall the information. Indeed, in a controlled laboratory setting, people surveyed after presidential debates are better able to recall the candidates' statements about issues that are personally important to them (Holbrook et al. 2005).

Alternatively, the relationship between knowledge and salience could be a product of reverse causality: learning factual information about an issue (correct or incorrect) leads people to care more about it. Identifying a causal relationship between personal relevance and inductive reasoning is almost impossible with observational data alone because when an issue is personally relevant, a person is not only more likely to engage in inductive reasoning around it but also to seek out and retain information about it (Holbrook et al. 2005).

Issue relevance and inductive reasoning

To determine whether people are more likely to engage in inductive reasoning around policies that are personally relevant, I experimentally manipulate the relevance of a policy. Because inductive reasoning is impossible to observe directly, the dependent variable of interest is a product of inductive reasoning: answers to closed-ended factual questions. The experiment tests the hypothesis that increasing a policy's personal relevance will decrease the number of "don't know" answers to factual questions about that policy.

The experiment was conducted in the summer of 2019 via the survey vendor Lucid. Lucid uses quota sampling to match U.S. census demographics, and participants recruited via Lucid perform similarly on several experimental benchmark surveys (Coppock and McClellan 2019). The survey was restricted to people between the ages of 22 and 62. First, all respondents were asked the year they were born, their gender, their educational attainment, and their level of political interest. They were also asked if they or anyone in their household currently collected Social Security benefits and how much they had heard about the future of the Social Security program.[2]

Participants were randomly assigned to either a treatment or control condition. In both, they read a brief news article describing a new government report about the Social Security program. Social Security was chosen as a policy focus for the study for two reasons. First, most people are somewhat familiar with the program (Barabas 2011). Second, compared to many other issues, fact-checking databases show that there is relatively little explicit misinformation. Between its launch and when the study was fielded in 2019, Politifact classified just 95 statements about Social Security (about nine per year) as false, mostly false, or "pants on fire." During this same time period, they classified 556 statements about immigration and 811 about healthcare as false, mostly false, or "pants on fire." None of the false Social Security statements included misinformation that corresponded to incorrect answers on the survey, and most of the statements consisted of misrepresentations of candidates' issue stances (e.g., "Mark Harris has said he would cut Social Security and Medicare" and "Rick Scott wants to destroy Social Security by privatizing it") rather than false information about the program itself.

The article read by participants in the treatment condition stated that a new government report predicted that benefits for people their age and older would be drastically reduced. Those in the control condition also learned that the benefits would be drastically reduced, but in their version of the article this reduction would only occur for people slightly *under* their current age (specifically, participants in the treatment condition were told that benefits would be reduced for people their age plus three, and those in the

New report: Social Security benefits at risk for those under 52

WASHINGTON, DC -- A new report from the bipartisan Joint Economic Committee estimates that millions of Americans currently under the age of 52 will receive drastically reduced Social Security benefits when they retire.

In late July, representatives Edward Handel (D-California) and Michael Barr (R-Texas), the heads of the committee, issued a statement expressing concern over Social Security's future. "What this report says is that just because someone had the bad luck to be born after 1967 they don't get to have a comfortable retirement. This is a major problem."

Mira Novkov, 49, currently earns $31,000 a year as a nurse practitioner and hopes to retire at 66. "This is completely unfair," she said about the report's projections. "People our age are already struggling to pay our bills, and now we also have to worry about what happens after we retire?"

The report's analyses conclude that people born before 1967 will receive their full benefit package, but those born after that year will see much smaller monthly checks.

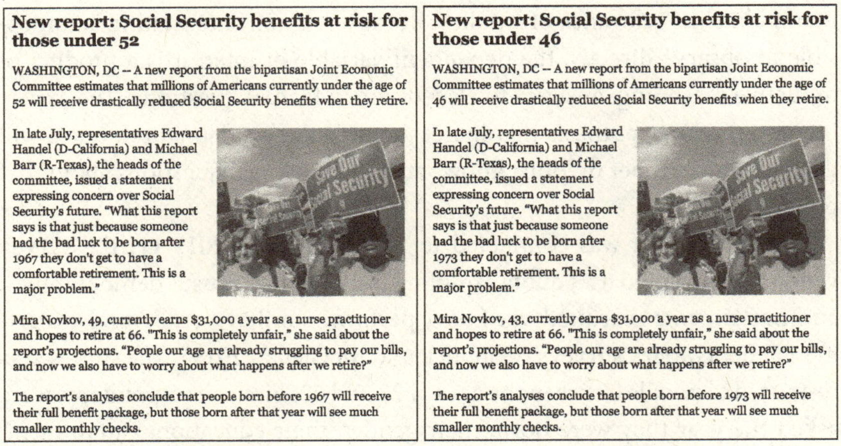

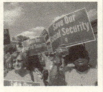

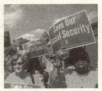

Treatment Version

New report: Social Security benefits at risk for those under 46

WASHINGTON, DC -- A new report from the bipartisan Joint Economic Committee estimates that millions of Americans currently under the age of 46 will receive drastically reduced Social Security benefits when they retire.

In late July, representatives Edward Handel (D-California) and Michael Barr (R-Texas), the heads of the committee, issued a statement expressing concern over Social Security's future. "What this report says is that just because someone had the bad luck to be born after 1973 they don't get to have a comfortable retirement. This is a major problem."

Mira Novkov, 43, currently earns $31,000 a year as a nurse practitioner and hopes to retire at 66. "This is completely unfair," she said about the report's projections. "People our age are already struggling to pay our bills, and now we also have to worry about what happens after we retire?"

The report's analyses conclude that people born before 1973 will receive their full benefit package, but those born after that year will see much smaller monthly checks.

Control Version

Figure 4.1 Example treatment vs. control article for a 49-year-old

control condition were told that benefits would be reduced for people their age minus three).

Figure 4.1 shows what the treatment and control versions would look like for a participant who said they were born in 1970 (making them approximately 49 years old at the time of the survey).

After reading the article, respondents were told that they should evaluate whether a series of factual statements about Social Security were true or false, and if they were not sure of the right answer, to select 'don't know.' They then evaluated seven statements about the program, presented in random order. The questions were based on past surveys assessing knowledge of Social Security (Cook et al. 2010; Barabas 2011). None of the answers were included in the article. The seven statements are below.

- If you begin collecting Social Security benefits early, you have to pay a penalty.
- Social Security benefits are tax-free.
- Social Security is not protected against inflation.
- Social Security is one of the top two federal budget expenses.
- Food stamps are funded through Social Security.
- The majority of the Social Security trust fund is invested in the stock market.
- Somebody who makes $150,000 pays as much in Social Security taxes as a millionaire.

Results: Relevance spurs inductive reasoning

A manipulation check, administered immediately after the treatment, asked respondents how much the results of the government report would affect them personally. In the treatment condition, the average response was 3.2 on a 4-point scale, while in the control condition, the average response was 2.1; a significant difference ($t = 11.6$, $p < .001$). Averaging across both conditions, respondents answered "don't know" to two out of the seven questions, answered three questions correctly, and answered two questions incorrectly.

This experiment was designed to test the hypothesis that when a policy becomes personally relevant, people are more likely to engage in inductive reasoning, and thus less likely to answer "don't know" to factual questions about that policy. Table 4.1 shows the effect of the treatment on the number of don't know answers, correct answers, and incorrect answers, with several demographic characteristics included as covariates.

Model 1 shows that the hypothesis is supported: people who were randomly assigned to believe that their Social Security would be reduced in the future (as opposed to benefits being reduced for people three years younger than them) were significantly less likely to answer "don't know" to factual questions about the policy. As with other surveys on political knowledge, women are more likely to answer "don't know," and people with higher levels of education and political interest are less likely (Dolan 2011; Luskin and Bullock 2011; Delli Carpini and Keeter 1996). Models 2 and 3 show that the treatment had no effect on correct answers but increased the number of incorrect answers that people gave. The treatment not only increased factual inferences, but also *incorrect* factual inferences.

The results show that people who come to believe that a policy is more personally relevant are less likely to answer "don't know" to factual questions about that policy. However, this experimental design cannot distinguish between two different potential mechanisms. The first is inductive reasoning: increased relevance leads people to make more factual inferences. The second is that increasing the personal relevance of Social Security causes them to engage in a more effortful memory search. Instead of inferring more facts, people could be recalling more facts (albeit some that are incorrect).[3]

This second possibility is certainly plausible, especially since people who self-reported having heard more about Social Security were also more likely to answer incorrectly. However, one of the reasons that I chose Social Security

Table 4.1 Effects of personal relevance on answers to factual questions

	(1) Don't know	(2) Correct	(3) Incorrect
Personal relevance	−0.47**	0.16	0.34**
	(0.18)	(0.14)	(0.12)
Female	0.53**	−0.21	−0.19
	(0.18)	(0.14)	(0.12)
Political interest	−0.59***	0.44***	0.21*
	(0.12)	(0.095)	(0.082)
Education	−0.23*	0.12	0.079
	(0.10)	(0.083)	(0.071)
Receive Social Security benefits	−0.42*	−0.0040	0.37**
	(0.20)	(0.16)	(0.14)
Heard about Social Security	−0.41***	0.12	0.27**
	(0.12)	(0.096)	(0.082)
Constant	5.30***	1.10**	0.37
	(0.44)	(0.35)	(0.30)
Observations	448	448	448
Adjusted R^2	0.176	0.082	0.096

Note: Standard errors in parentheses
*$p < 0.05$, **$p < 0.01$, ***$p < 0.001$

as an issue is the relative infrequency of explicit misinformation about the program—in particular, misinformation that would be relevant to the factual questions asked in this survey. While of course it is possible that people encountered misinformation about Social Security in places not tracked by PolitiFact, the lack of systematic misinformation increases the likelihood that at least some of the decrease in "don't know" answers is a product of inductive reasoning rather than of recalling false information.

The question of whether the factual answers that people provide are a product of inference or recall parallels a similar argument over how people answer opinion questions on surveys: do they "*construct* attitudes from ideas they can retrieve from memory as they are questioned [or] *recall* attitudes formed at an earlier time" (Zaller and Feldman 1992, 592). Zaller and Feldman present evidence that at least when it comes to opinions, people both construct *and* recall. Indeed, forcing a discrete choice between inference and recall is an oversimplification of the complicated cognitive processes involved in answering a knowledge question. It is quite possible—and even likely—that both processes occur simultaneously, both in the real world and in this experiment.

Work in cognitive psychology directly testing whether memory (specifically recognition memory) is a fundamentally different process from induction concludes that they are not: "Although 'recognition' and 'induction' may be useful task descriptions . . . these labels do not necessarily map onto fundamental distinctions in human cognition" (Hayes and Heit 2013, 792). While Zaller and Feldman published their piece more than a decade earlier, their conclusion is consistent with these empirical findings, suggesting that attitudes (as expressed in surveys) are neither constructed entirely on the spot or purely a product of recall; rather, they are a combination of both processes. Our factual knowledge may not be so different from our opinions. Facts, like opinions, are constructed from a combination of memory, inference, and context.

This experiment offers evidence for a causal link between personal relevance and inductive reasoning in the policy realm. This link is intuitively plausible given that relevance also spurs people to seek out information from external sources. This finding has several implications for understanding what people know (and get wrong) about politics and policy.

First, we should expect that when policies are perceived as more personally relevant, people will engage in more inductive reasoning about them. The word "perceived" matters quite a lot, because elites often have an interest in convincing voters that a particular policy is personally relevant, even if by objective standards it may not be. For example, during his 2016 campaign, Donald Trump emphasized how immigration could affect Americans' personal and economic safety (Sides et al. 2019). During and after the campaign, the number of people who believed immigration was a problem rose steadily, and in 2019 the number of people citing immigration as the country's "most important problem" rose to its highest level (Jones 2019).

Second, inductive reasoning does not inevitably lead to the creation of misperceptions. Whether someone makes a correct or incorrect factual inference about a policy or issue will depend on a number of factors, both on the individual level (e.g., partisanship and related knowledge) and on the policy level (e.g., the volume and content of media coverage).

Finally, personal relevance is likely not the only catalyst for inductive reasoning. Information can also have *social* utility (Chaffee and McLeod 1973). In an experimental context, when people are told that they will be asked to participate in a discussion about a particular topic, they are more likely to seek out information about that topic (Atkin 1972), and survey research shows that people often provide social reasons for their news consumption, for example, "to give me something to talk about with others" (Kaye and Johnson 2002). Thus, when people expect to engage in discussion about a particular issue, they may be more likely to engage in inductive reasoning about it, in addition to seeking out information externally.

Inductive reasoning and policy misperceptions

This section investigates the question of *how* inductive reasoning can produce policy misperceptions. In psychology, much of the experimental research around inductive reasoning employs highly stylized scenarios, often about animal taxonomy. For example, what strategies do people use to infer that if lions have sharp teeth, then tigers probably do too? I draw on these studies to shed light on how people make factual inferences about a slightly more complicated topic: public policy.

A first step in understanding how inductive reasoning can create misperceptions is to observe the factual beliefs that people articulate spontaneously, without the structuring of closed-ended questions. In the following section, I first look for patterns of misperceptions in open-ended responses to factual questions. Then, I draw on psychology research to outline the strategies of inductive reasoning that may have led to these conclusions. The goal of these explanations is to offer insight into how the inductive strategies that people use to make inferences about policies may lead them astray. For each of the topics listed in Table 4.2, I use open-ended questions to identify

Table 4.2 Overview of open-ended studies

Issue	Recruitment	Size	Date
Social Security	Lucid	748	2019
Refugees	Mechanical Turk	400	2019
National debt	SSI	383	2015

common misperceptions, then discuss how particular types of inductive reasoning may have created them.

I draw on open-ended rather than closed-ended questions for the same reasons that, in Chapter 1, I employ interviews. Open-ended questions make it possible to identify what people believe absent any preconceptions of what they *should* believe (Lupia 2006). Because these are observational data, it is impossible to definitively trace a given misperception to its source, be it inductive reasoning, a misleading Facebook post, or some combination of the two. But again, the reality is that drawing a bright line between recall and induction is an unnecessary and likely misleading dichotomization of how human cognition works. The facts we generate via inductive reasoning are not invented from whole cloth; rather, they are woven together from our experiences, related knowledge, and logical reasoning. The goal of this book is to understand how all of those factors work together to create systematic misperceptions about public policy.

Social Security and attributions of intentionality

In total, 748 respondents recruited via Lucid were asked, "What is the major reason that Social Security is facing financial difficulties? If you're not sure of the answer, you can type 'not sure.'" Overall, 39% of respondents answered some variant of "not sure," and the rest offered an explanation. These 481 substantive answers were coded into five categories. Table 4.3 shows the categories, distribution, and examples of these responses.

The modal response was fundamentally correct in attributing the program's difficulties to demographic shifts.[4] The rest of the responses were less obviously accurate. About one in five respondents stated that Social Security was in trouble because the government had diverted funds from Social Security to pay for other programs, ranging from the general ("other things," "other uses," "other areas") to the specific ("to pay for the deficit," "raises for themselves," "the stupid wall"). Fifteen percent of respondents attributed the program's issues to "bad management" on the part of the government. Finally, 12% suggested that people were defrauding the Social Security system, and 12% said that the economy as a whole was responsible for Social Security's financial issues.

While answers that attribute Social Security's problems to demographic shifts come closest to an accurate description of the issue, answers in other

Table 4.3 Explanations offered in open-ended responses for Social Security's financial difficulties

Belief	Frequency	Examples
Demographics	38% (184)	• People are living longer, and they are having to pay out more to the elderly now • More being taken out than being put in • The baby boomers have used all the money
Diverted funds	22% (105)	• The funding has been used for other purposes • The government dipping into the funds for other things like raises for themselves • Because the government takes money out to fund other things: Obama care, etc.
Bad management	15% (75)	• The government's lack of efforts of leadership of taking care of the elderly • In general our country's finances are grossly mishandled • Bad money management
Fraud	12% (58)	• People that don't really need it are taking advantage • Because people are scamming • A lot of people that are on Social Security do not need it; they are fooling the system
The economy	12% (59)	• The economy is in flux • Inflation—takes more money to survive • The economy is getting bad

categories are not necessarily incompatible with an accurate understanding. For example, a person who answered "bad management" could know that changing demographics had jeopardized Social Security but also believe that the government has failed to address those changing dynamics. However, the goal of this study is not to precisely distinguish between "correct" and "incorrect" assertions; rather, it is to understand how inductive reasoning might lead people to favor certain types of explanations.

Instead of offering an explanation that blames demographic change or larger economic conditions, a third of respondents attribute the program's problems to purposeful actions on the part of either the government (misusing funds) or citizens (committing fraud). Together, these categories make up 34% of the substantive responses—about the same proportion as correct answers.

Both the "bad management" and "fraud" explanations rely on the same inferential strategy, that is, a person infers that an ambiguous event was most likely motivated by *intentional action* on the part of someone else (Rosset 2008). Humans are fundamentally wired to understand phenomena as motivated by intentional actions rather than by random chance or systemic regularities (Hilton 2017). For example, stock analysts tend to attribute random variation in stock prices to specific events (Taleb 2005). In social interactions, when people observe something good (or bad) happening to someone else, they often causally attribute this outcome to the person's moral character, even when that causal connection is impossible (Callan et al. 2014). In addition, humans are more likely to perceive intention when an outcome is negative rather than positive (Knobe 2004). Overall, the responses suggest that explanations as to why Social Security is facing financial trouble may be influenced by the tendency to infer intentionality.

This distinction between assigning blame to an individual versus a system echoes a point made by Iyengar (1994), who argues that part of understanding a particular issue involves assigning responsibility. The parallel is not exact, as Iyengar focuses on how people come to attribute responsibility for larger social problems (crime, poverty, unemployment) rather than specific policy outcomes. However, his observation that people (both journalists and the public) have an instinctive tendency to understand problems as "idiosyncratic outcomes" rather than "deep-seated social or economic conditions" (p. 137) is echoed in these open-ended responses.

Refugees and misleading rhetoric

This study examined knowledge of (and misperceptions about) the differences between a refugee and an immigrant. In total, 400 respondents were asked to explain why the U.S. government classifies some people as "refugees" and some as "immigrants." Overall, about 10% of respondents did not answer or said they did not know. Of the 351 respondents who provided substantive answers, 78% gave an answer that was largely correct in explaining that refugees were people fleeing violence or persecution. However, 11% (39) said that the U.S. classified people as refugees if they tried to enter the United States illegally. Some examples of these responses are as follows:

- Immigrants are the people who enter our country officially, and refugees are the persons who enter our country in a wrong way.

- Immigrants are people who can legally enter our country. Refuges are those people who are hidden and illegally enter our country.
- Refugees come illegally.
- They are called refugees because they enter into the country illegally.

Education and political interest were both negatively associated with the belief that "refugee" was a synonym for "illegal." However, the misperception was unrelated to partisanship. Republicans were no more likely than Democrats and Independents to provide this answer, suggesting that it is not simply a product of expressive responding or "partisan cheerleading" (Schaffner and Luks 2018).

The incorrect inference that "refugees" is a synonym for "undocumented immigrant" may be shaped by then-President Trump's rhetoric about refugees, which often suggested that refugees were dangerous and even criminal (Scribner 2017). For example, in November 2017, he tweeted: "ISIS is taking credit for the terrible stabbing attack at Ohio State University by a Somali refugee who should not have been in our country." Given Trump's consistent characterization of refugees as criminals, the inference that they are criminal partly because they have entered the United States illegally makes some sense.

These results illustrate how misleading elite rhetoric can lead to incorrect inferences even in the absence of explicit misinformation (Jerit and Barabas 2006). Fact-checking organizations like Politifact do not have a record of President Trump explicitly providing an incorrect definition of refugees as "people who enter the United States illegally." However, because he consistently characterized refugees as criminals, people may have drawn on this information to infer that the definition of refugee is "someone who has committed a criminal act" —in this case, crossing the border illegally.

The national debt and taxonomic similarity

In the previous two studies, participants were explicitly asked to answer a question about a policy-current fact. In this study, participants were asked to draw on their existing knowledge to make predictions about the future. Specifically, they were asked the open-ended question: "What are the consequences (if any) of the national debt?"

Fourteen percent of respondents answered some version of "not sure" or "don't know." The 304 substantive responses were coded into four categories. Nearly half (43%) predicted internal financial difficulty for the United States, ranging from general ("the economy will collapse") to specific ("we might not have enough money to keep funding things like new roads"). Another 35% were concerned about how the debt would affect the ability of the United States to participate in the global economy ("credibility as a nation goes down," "lose its place as being one of the top powers in the global market," "other countries will stop doing business with us"). Six percent were confident that nothing at all would happen. Finally, 16% (47) expressed highly specific concerns about other countries (most frequently China) "taking over" or repossessing parts of the United States. A few representative quotes illustrating this belief include the following:

- China will eventually start to demand more and more and eventually try to take over the United States if it gets bad enough.
- I truly believe that eventually you will see the Chinese national symbol somewhere on our dollar bills.
- China will eventually get tired of us owing them money, and they will take over our country.
- The country will be foreclosed on and its assets sold at auction, causing the country as we know it to cease to exist.

People who hold the belief that China (or other countries) will be able to "collect" on debt by taking over parts of the country may be making inferences via an inductive strategy called "taxonomic similarity." Drawing on taxonomic similarity means generalizing category properties from another item that falls in the same category. For example, if you are asked to describe a "pizzly bear," you might draw on your knowledge of grizzly bears and polar bears, under the assumption that all members of category "bear" share similar properties (Osherson et al. 1990).[5]

Similarly, when people are asked to make inferences about the national debt, they draw on their knowledge of other things that fall into the larger category of "debt." One of the first that comes to mind is personal or household debt. Not only is this analogy personally salient, but it is also reinforced in elite rhetoric, like President Obama's 2011 statement that "families across this country understand what it takes to manage a budget. Well, it's time Washington acted as responsibly as our families do" (Craighead 2011).

When an individual or household carries a debt, they usually owe it to an external creditor like a bank or a credit card company, who are legally allowed to collect unpaid debt by confiscating items like a car, home, or personal property. So, generalizing from household debt leads people to infer that items in the category "debt" have the characteristic "failure to repay can legally allow the creditor to repossess property." However, this analogy leads to incorrect inferences because the national debt is fundamentally different from household debt (Krugman 2012).

Participants in the survey were also asked to estimate the percentage of the national debt held by four different entities: China, Japan, the Federal Reserve, and Social Security.[6] Among people whose open-ended responses predicted that other countries would repossess parts of the U.S., 82% estimated that the two foreign countries held more of the debt than domestic entities. In contrast, among those who gave answers in the other categories, only 50% incorrectly estimated the relative amount of debt held. This misperception may be attributable to the same strategy of inductive reasoning: assuming that "household debt" and "national debt" are members of the same category, and therefore that debt must be held by external creditors.

These responses illustrate how taxonomic similarity, one of the most common strategies of inductive reasoning, can create policy misperceptions. This strategy could also help explain misperceptions around other policies that have similar names but very different implementation strategies and beneficiaries: for example, farm subsidies (money paid to farmers and owners of farmland) versus corporate relocation subsidies (tax breaks given to companies to encourage them to do business in a particular place).

Conclusion

How do people come to hold factual beliefs about a policy? Often it is through learning: watching the news, talking politics with a friend, or reading a campaign mailer. Much of the existing research into political knowledge has been devoted to understanding how people learn about the political world from these and other external sources (Barabas et al. 2014; Dowling et al. 2020; Chaffee and Kanihan 1997; Bode 2016). However, people also move from ignorance to knowledge by engaging in inductive reasoning.

Inductive reasoning is an essential part of how we navigate the world. The key difference between inductive reasoning and other types of cognition is that "inductive processes produce a net increase in knowledge . . . they produce new but inevitably uncertain knowledge" (Bisanz et al. 1994, 182). This chapter draws on experimental and observational data to answer two questions. First, why do people engage in inductive reasoning around some policies but not others? And second, how can inductive reasoning create misperceptions? Evidence from an experiment suggests that when people perceive an issue has more personal relevance, they are more likely to make factual inferences about that issue, and the responses to open-ended questions about policies illustrate some of the inductive strategies that may create those inferences.

A recurring theme throughout the chapter is the difficulty of distinguishing between facts that are the products of learning/recall and those that are a product of inductive processes. The reality is that if we could peer inside a person's head, we would not find tidily sorted piles labeled "information I learned" and "information I invented." Rather, most of what we think of as "knowledge" is an often-messy combination of information, belief, and logical reasoning:

> Most knowledge is little more than a bunch of associations, high-level links between objects or people that aren't broken down into detailed stories . . . on most subjects, we connect only abstract bits of information, and what we know is little more than a feeling of understanding we can't really unpack. (Sloman and Fernbach 2018, 10)

The lesson from this chapter is that what people know—and get wrong—about policy is driven not only by what they see in the world but also by internal cognitive processes, including inference and even imagination (Petersen and Aarøe 2013). This observation has real implications for how agenda-setting might shape not only issue salience but also factual beliefs. Substantial evidence suggests that the more the media cover an issue, the more people perceive that issue to be important. Instinctively, we might assume that when a new issue appears on the agenda, it means that people will be ignorant about it until the media or political elites provide relevant factual information. But the experiment in this chapter shows that people can and will fill in the blanks themselves.

Partisanship, and in particular partisan-driven motivated reasoning, is largely absent from this chapter. A substantial literature shows that our partisan identities shape our factual beliefs (Swire et al. 2017; Flynn et al. 2017;

Lodge and Taber 2013; Berinsky 2017). But in most of the examples in this chapter, partisanship is not associated with misperceptions. This pattern should not be taken as evidence that partisanship never matters for policy misperceptions; rather, it is a reminder that there are many government policies and programs that have been only minimally politicized, often because both parties largely agree on them and/or they have not been subject to recent political debate (Mettler 2011; Bennett 1996b). When it comes to making inferences about these policies, partisanship may simply not be a particularly useful heuristic.

An important outstanding question is the extent to which misperceptions formed by inductive reasoning are *different* than those formed by exposure to misinformation. Again, it is helpful to think of these issues through the lens of Zaller and Feldman's (1992) model of survey response. In their model, attitudes have a "central tendency and a variance." Constructed beliefs are similar. The specific belief that refugees are defined as "people who have entered the country illegally" may not always be stable over multiple survey waves, but the larger pattern of inductive reasoning that led to that belief is likely to produce similar responses. Indeed, Graham (2023) finds that even confidently held misperceptions (e.g., about the unemployment rate and economic growth) are less stable over time than confidently held true beliefs. This makes sense if many misperceptions are constructed from heuristics and reasoning rather than a result of direct exposure to misinformation.

But as discussed in Chapter 1, if we re-center this discussion on citizen competence, our fundamental concern should not just be the stability of false beliefs are or even how certain people are of their accuracy. Both of those attributes matter largely because we intuit that they are associated with something much more important. If a false belief is more stable or held with more certainty, we suspect it might be more likely to threaten democratic competence—in other words, to affect attitudes. But this is, of course, an empirical question, and one that I take up in Chapter 5.

5
How people interpret policy information

The previous chapters identified widely held policy misperceptions and investigated how they arise. This chapter, along with Chapter 6, takes on another question: Do policy misperceptions actually matter for attitudes and/or behavior? In Chapter 1, I argued that a false belief does not inevitably threaten democratic accountability. With some false beliefs, this disconnect is obvious: someone can believe that unicorns roam the Nebraska plains without it affecting their vote. But our intuition about what "matters" is harder to trust when it comes to false beliefs that are directly about politics. What about the misperceptions that Hillary Clinton is involved in a sex-trafficking ring or that the unemployment rate is much higher than it really is? It seems intuitively plausible that if we could wave a magic wand and erase those misperceptions, people would like Clinton more and evaluate the economy more positively. But in practice, even when people accept factual corrections about politics, their attitudes often remain stubbornly the same.

As Chapter 1 discussed, the question of how beliefs shape attitudes lies at the heart of democratic competence. Fundamentally, we are concerned about misperceptions to the extent that they threaten people's ability to make political decisions that are in line with their underlying values and interests. These threats to democratic competence may take many forms, like a person voting for a ballot initiative they would otherwise oppose, rejecting a candidate they would otherwise prefer, or prioritizing an issue they would otherwise ignore. However, simply noting an association between a particular misperception and related attitude or behavior is not sufficient to demonstrate that the first *caused* the second: as Brendan Nyhan (2020, 223) concisely explains, "we lack a systematic understanding for when factual beliefs are the basis for a preference versus a rationalization for a preference that a respondent would hold anyway."

Given the difficulties of establishing causality via observational data, experiments are critical for exploring these counterfactuals. Experiments make it possible to identify causal relationships between misperceptions and attitudes (or alternatively, as often makes more sense for both ethical and practical reasons, *corrections* and attitudes). Randomly assigning some people to receive corrections makes it possible to directly measure whether correcting misperceptions has downstream effects on attitudes.

This book is far from the first to use experiments to examine the attitudinal impact of factual corrections. The next section begins with a systematic overview of ten studies that use experiments to test the impact of 14 different policy-related factual corrections on both beliefs and attitudes. For each study, I describe the type of information provided in the correction (policy-current or policy-outcome), the post-treatment attitudinal measure, and whether the correction changed attitudes compared to the control group. The pattern of results shows that most policy attitudes are remarkably unmoved by corrective information. Across a range of studies, correcting misperceptions about facts like the unemployment rate, proportion of immigrants, and inflation has no effect on downstream attitudes.

This chapter offers an explanation for this difference: policy-outcome information (the subject of most of these corrective interventions) is particularly subject to partisan rationalization (Gaines et al. 2007; Bisgaard 2015). People interpret policy-outcome information through a partisan lens; thereby using it to reinforce rather than change their attitudes. I argue that, in contrast, policy-current information may be less subject to this type of partisan interpretation.

I test this theory in an experiment measuring the extent to which people perceive policy-current facts vs. policy-outcome facts to have partisan implications. Across ten different issues, participants consistently rate facts about policy *outcomes* (e.g., the percent of people who are uninsured or the change in tax rates) as more politicized than facts about *current* policy (e.g., the Medicare eligibility age or the existing tax rate).

Finally, I directly compare the downstream attitudinal effects of policy-outcome versus policy-current corrections on a specific issue: refugee policy. Corrective information about existing refugee policies substantially increases support for refugees as compared to corrective information about refugee-related policy outcomes (e.g., the proportion of refugees who receive welfare benefits).

Can corrections change attitudes?

The question of whether a correction can change *attitudes* is very different from the question of whether that correction can change *beliefs*, although the two are often conflated. This section summarizes a range of studies that have examined the effects of corrections on attitudes through experimental designs in which participants are randomly assigned to receive factual information aimed at correcting a specific misperception. Then, both the beliefs and attitudes of participants are measured.[1]

An implicit assumption of many of these studies is that facts *should* change attitudes, and a failure to do so is characterized as "resistance." But it may be perfectly reasonable for a single fact to be insufficient evidence for updating an attitude, especially when that attitude is strongly held. Imagine, for example, a person who supports charter schools and mistakenly believes that they produce substantially more successful students. A family member of theirs had a positive experience sending a child to a charter school, and their own child has received poor support in public school. Then, this person is informed that, contrary to their beliefs, there is no systematic evidence that charter schools produce better outcomes for the students who attend them. It is not clear that this one correction—even if they fully accept it—*should* change their attitude about charter schools in the face of their lived experience. It is important not to take the failure of a particular correction to alter attitudes as evidence of people willfully ignoring factual information. In some cases the information may simply be insufficient to alter long-standing attitudes.

Table 5.1 summarizes ten studies selected from the literature on correction effects. The studies were included based on two criteria. First, the corrective interventions had to be about policy rather than partisan politics or politicians. I omitted studies that examined the attitudinal impact of correcting candidate-related misperceptions (e.g., Thorson 2016; Nyhan et al. 2019) or of political information not about policy (e.g., Williamson 2020). Second, the dependent variable had to tap attitudes directly related to that policy. I also omitted studies that examined the impact of corrective policy information on non-policy attitudes (e.g., affective polarization).

For each study, the table shows (1) the corrective information participants were given in the experiment, (2) whether that information is policy-current or policy-outcome, (3) the policy attitudes that served as the dependent variable, and (4) the information's effect on those policy attitudes.

Table 5.1 Studies examining the effects of corrections on policy attitudes

Study	Info type	Information	Attitude	Effect
Sides (2016)	Policy-current	% of people who pay the estate tax	Support for estate tax	Positive
Scotto et al. (2017)	Policy-current	% of federal budget going to foreign aid	Support for cutting foreign aid	Negative
Gilens (2001)	Policy-current	% of federal budget going to foreign aid	Support for cutting foreign aid	Negative
Kuklinski et al. (2000)	Policy-current	% of federal budget going to welfare	Support for cutting welfare and imposing a 2-year limit on payments	Negative
Berinsky (2007)	Policy-current	Cost of Iraq War	Support for the Iraq War	None
Gilens (2001)	Policy-outcome	Trend in crime rate	Support for prison spending	Negative
Hopkins, Sides, and Citrin (2019)	Policy-outcome	% of Americans that are foreign born	Support for increasing immigration	None
Howell, West, and Peterson (2011)	Policy-outcome	Average teacher salary	Support for higher teacher pay	Negative
Porter, Wood, and Bahador (2019)	Policy-outcome	Ice caps are at record low level	Support for tougher environmental regulation	None
Lawrence and Sides (2014)	Policy-outcome	Median income and educational attainment in the U.S.	Support for student loans, aid to the poor, and job training	None
Lawrence and Sides (2014)	Policy-outcome	Racial composition of U.S. population	Support for govt spending to help Blacks, affirmative action, and immigration	None
Lawrence and Sides (2014)	Policy-outcome	Unemployment and poverty rates	Support for loans for college tuition, aid to the poor, job training, unemployment benefits, and food stamps	None
Grigorieff, Roth, and Ubfal (2020)	Policy-outcome	% of immigrants in the U.S., no. of undocumented, immigrant employment and incarceration rate	Index of immigrant-friendly policy preferences	None
Berinsky (2007)	Policy-outcome	Casualties in the Iraq War	Support for the Iraq War	None

Among these studies, the impact of policy-outcome information is tested more than twice as often as policy-current information. It makes intuitive sense that scholars have focused on examining how providing people with information about the *outcomes* of policy change attitudes given the importance of retrospective voting to democratic accountability. Retrospective voting suggests that people need not know the ins and outs of policy; they need only look to their own personal experience ("pocketbook voting") or the welfare of people around them ("sociotropic voting"). People who believe that the incumbent government has done a good job managing the economy, war, and other areas are then more likely to reward them with their vote (Healy and Malhotra 2013). Policy-outcome information thus allows people to evaluate government performance in a way that policy-current information may not.

In all of these studies described in Table 5.1, facts succeeded in changing beliefs, suggesting that people are in general quite willing to update their beliefs in light of new information (Wood and Porter 2019; Porter and Wood 2019). However, across seven of the nine experiments that randomly assign people to receive corrective information on the outcomes of policies, including the proportion of immigrants, war casualty rates, and the crime rate, the information fails to affect policy attitudes. In contrast, four out of the five studies that give participants information about existing policies do succeed in changing attitudes. There is a puzzle here. Outcome information seems like it should be an efficient way for voters to evaluate policy. Why, then, does it so often fail to affect attitudes? As a step toward solving this puzzle, the following section maps out how people process factual information about politics and integrate it into their existing attitudes and beliefs.

How people process factual information

What happens when someone encounters a new piece of information? How do they decide whether to believe it and how do they integrate it into their existing attitudes? Gaines et al. (2007) outline a theory of how people respond to new factual information. They propose differentiating between beliefs, interpretations, and opinions. Interpretations are the mediating step between beliefs and opinions—for example, one person might interpret a particular tax rate as high, while another might interpret it as low. In their taxonomy, "complete updating" takes place when a person accepts a new piece of information, alters their interpretations, and then updates their related opinions accordingly.

Gaines et al. propose that even when people believe a particular fact, it can fail to shape their opinions, for one of two reasons. The first is via an "opinion disconnect," in which pre-existing opinions are strong enough that even a new piece of disconfirmatory information fails to change them. For example, an ardent opponent of Donald Trump may not revise their negative opinion of him even after learning that unemployment decreased during his first year in office. The second way that facts can fail to affect opinions is through "meaning avoidance," in which a person interprets a particular fact in a way that is consistent with their pre-existing opinions.

However, it is worth noting that the term "avoidance" implies that there is a "correct" way to interpret a fact, which is often not the case. For example, each year since 2015, police in American have fatally shot about 1,000 people. Someone who is supportive of the police may interpret this as evidence that, contrary to popular narrative, police shootings are not increasing, and thus the increased attention to police violence is unwarranted. Someone who is skeptical of the police may interpret this as evidence that police violence is continuing unchecked and reform is critical. Neither person is necessarily avoiding a "correct" interpretation—rather, there are multiple plausible interpretations of the same fact, and people tend to gravitate toward ones that support their pre-existing opinions. Still, Gaines et al.'s (2007) recognition that interpretations necessarily mediate the relationship between facts and opinions is an important contribution, which suggests that differences in how people *interpret* policy-current versus policy-outcome facts may help explain their divergent effects on attitudes.

Bisgaard (2019) investigates this process of interpretation through both experiments and open-ended questions. He finds that even when partisans accept the same facts about economic outcomes, they interpret those facts in ways that reinforce their pre-existing views, attributing responsibility for positive outcomes to their preferred party and for negative outcomes to their not preferred party. The results suggest that "although partisans might acknowledge new facts, the mere acknowledgment of these facts apparently leads them to reason about the question of responsibility in a highly partisan-motivated fashion" (Bisgaard 2019, 15).

Carlson (2019) finds a similar pattern in a different context. When asked to summarize a news article about economic performance, Republicans and Democrats conveyed similar basic facts, but interpreted those facts in ways that reinforced their partisan predispositions. While it might be tempting to dismiss these divergent interpretations as partisan-driven motivated reasoning, the fact that partisans respond differently to the same piece of information is also consistent with Bayesian updating. Because Democrats and Republicans have different types of existing knowledge and experience, they are likely to interpret any given fact differently (Coppock 2023).

In summary, people interpret factual information based on their predispositions (including but not limited to partisanship) and knowledge. Whether or not a piece of new information has downstream effects on attitude depends on that interpretation. The puzzle, however, remains: Why is it that across the studies in Table 5.1, facts about policy *outcomes* seem to be less effective at changing attitudes than facts about *existing* policy? One potential explanation for this pattern is that, consistent with Bisgaard (2019), people interpret policy-outcome facts in a way that reinforces their pre-existing partisan beliefs. The next section presents the results of a study designed to answer two related questions. First, do people see policy-outcome facts as more politicized than policy-current facts? And if so, what potential processes of interpretation might contribute to this pattern?

Study 1: Partisan implications of policy facts

This survey experiment was designed to (1) test the hypothesis that people are more likely to engage in partisan interpretation of policy-outcome facts than policy-current facts and (2) explore the thoughts that people generate in response to policy-current versus policy-outcome facts.

Study 1 design

In this experiment, participants read a series of factual statements. Each described either an aspect of a current policy or an outcome of that policy. After reading each statement, they then assessed how likely it was that the statement was made by a partisan actor.

Before explaining the experimental design in more detail, I note that this design differs from a typical survey experiment in an important way. In many experiments, maintaining informational equivalence is a primary goal (Dafoe et al. 2018). That goal is by definition unattainable here since this study's purpose is to directly compare how people react to different types of information.

The lack of informational equivalence means that we should be especially concerned that any observed difference is actually due to the vagaries of a particular issue or set of facts rather than a result of how people process policy-outcome versus policy-current information (Druckman 2022). For example, imagine that respondents characterized policy-outcome information about healthcare as more partisan than policy-current information about healthcare. This pattern could plausibly be because healthcare is a uniquely politicized issue, or because of the particular set of facts I chose, rather than because of inherent differences in how people process policy-outcome vs. policy-current information.

I take several steps to address this issue. First, to increase the ability to generalize beyond a particular issue area, I compare policy-current and policy-outcome information across ten separate issues (20 facts in all). The full set of facts is shown in Table 5.2. Second, to address concerns about bias in choosing facts, when possible I chose policy-current and policy-outcome facts that had been used as information treatments in previous studies. In total, six out of the ten policy-current statements and five out of the ten policy-outcome statements were used in previous studies. These statements are noted with an asterisk in Table 5.2.

In total, 1,828 respondents were recruited via the online survey platform Lucid in the spring of 2021. After answering several demographic questions, they were told, "Next, you will see ten statements about politics and policy that have recently been in the news. Please read each statement carefully, and then give your best guess at who made the statement: a Democrat or a Republican. If it seems like it could have been made by either a Republican or Democrat, select 'Equally likely to be a Democrat or Republican.'" Then, they were randomly assigned to see either a fact about existing policy or one about a policy outcome for each of ten different issues: healthcare, food stamps, immigration, education, taxes, Temporary Assistance for Needy Families (TANF), refugees, the national debt, Social Security, and the environment. Each person evaluated five policy-outcome statements and five policy-current statements.

At the end of the survey, they were randomly assigned to see one of the ten statements that they did *not* evaluate in the first part of the experiment

Table 5.2 Policy-current and policy-outcome facts used in Study 1

Issue area	Policy-current information	Policy-outcome information
Healthcare	By law health insurance companies are not allowed to charge people more money because they have a pre-existing condition.	The percentage of people without health insurance in the U.S. has decreased.
Food stamps	Undocumented immigrants are not eligible for food stamps.*	Since 2016, the percentage of Americans who receive food stamps has declined.
Immigration	U.S. policy places a limit on how many immigrants can come to the United States from any one country each year.	The crime rate among immigrants is lower than the crime rate among native-born U.S. citizens.*
Education	About a third of funding for schools is based on property taxes.	Black children are more than twice as likely as white children to attend a high-poverty school.
Taxes	A person who makes over $500,000 a year is required to pay 37% of their income in taxes.*	Today, the extremely wealthy pay less in taxes than they did 50 years ago.
TANF	There is a federal limit on how long people can receive TANF (welfare) benefits.*	About 23% of families living in poverty receive TANF (welfare) benefits.*
Refugees	Refugees to the United States are required to undergo background checks.*	About 14% of refugees receive welfare benefits or food stamps.*
Debt	Most of the national debt is owed to the Federal Reserve.*	Over the last four years, the national debt has increased.
Social Security	Social Security benefits are paid for by taxes on people who are currently employed.*	The amount of money in the Social Security trust fund is decreasing.
Environment	The Clean Air Act regulates emissions from manufacturing to limit hazardous air pollution.	Ice caps are currently at record low levels.*

*Corrective information has been previously used in a study in this book or elsewhere

and asked an open-ended question: "Finally, please just take a moment to tell us what you think of the statement below." This question was designed to provide more insight into the thoughts generated by the factual statements, and how they might differ across policy-current and policy-outcome facts.

Study 1 results: Partisan interpretation of policy-outcome vs. policy-current information

I recode each response into a 0–2 scale, ranging from 0 ("equally likely to have been made by a Democrat or Republican") to 2 ("very likely a [Republican/ Democrat] made the statement"). I collapse across party lines because for the purposes of testing whether policy-current facts are more subject to partisan interpretation than policy-outcome facts, it is the presence of perceived partisanship that matters rather than its direction.

First, I examine what types of people are more likely to perceive policy information—regardless of whether it is policy-current or policy-outcome—as partisan. Figure 5.1 presents the results of a regression predicting the average score across all ten facts.

Strong partisans and those who are politically interested are significantly more likely to perceive the statements as being made by partisan actors. Their political awareness makes it easier for them to infer "what goes with what," politically speaking, and therefore to interpret new information through a partisan lens. These positive associations with political interest and

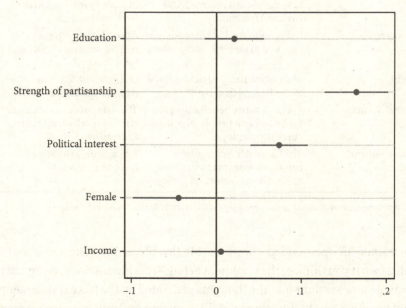

Figure 5.1 Factors associated with perceptions of facts as more partisan (0-2 scale)

partisanship suggest that the measure of perceived partisanship employed in the survey does indeed capture meaningful variation in perceptions.

The primary hypothesis motivating this study was that people will infer that policy-outcome statements are more likely to have been made by partisan actors than policy-current statements. Figure 5.2 shows the average perceived partisanship for the policy-current versus policy-outcome fact in each issue area. For nine out of the ten issues, respondents perceive the policy-outcome statement as significantly more likely to have been made by a partisan actor than the policy-current statement. The only exception is the issue of food stamps.

Across all ten issues, the policy-outcome facts receive a score of .84, compared to 1.2 for the policy-outcome facts. Overall, respondents believed that the policy-outcome facts were substantially more likely to have been made by a partisan than the policy-current facts, suggesting that people are indeed more likely see policy-outcome facts as reflecting partisan considerations.

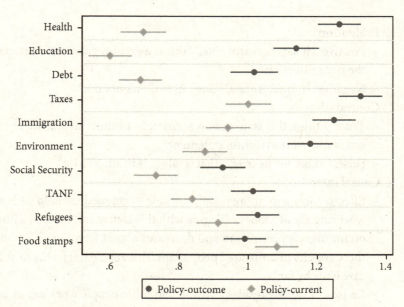

Figure 5.2 Average belief that a statement was made by a partisan actor (0–2 scale)

Study 1 results: Interpretation of policy information

At the end of the survey, each person was asked to reflect on one of the facts that they did not evaluate as part of the first part of the study. I draw on these open-ended responses to investigate what types of thoughts people generated in response to policy-current versus policy-outcome information.

Prior to collecting the responses, I created four non-mutually-exclusive dimensions along which to code each answer. The dimensions were designed to capture the primary ways that people might interpret the information. The first dimension measures whether the participant expressed positive or negative sentiments about the information. The second codes for evaluations of the statement's veracity. The third captures processes of causal inference: each statement was coded for whether it brought up a potential *cause* of the fact or a potential *effect* of the fact.

Finally, each statement was coded based on the schema proposed by Lodge and Taber (2013) as either "bolstering" (whether the respondent presents an argument for why the statement is credible or worth believing) or "denigrating" (whether the respondent presents an argument for why the statement is not credible or not worth believing). The following list provides an overview of the categories and examples of several statements in each.

1. **Evaluation**
   - Positive: "it seems reasonable," "this is a good regulation," "a step in the right direction."
   - Negative: "I think it's sad," "don't like it," "it's not fair."
2. **Contestation**
   - True: "I think this statement is accurate," "I think this statement is a sad truth," "it is a truthful statement."
   - False: "This can't be true," "that is false," "I think it's a lie."
3. **Causal inference**
   - Effects: "now a lot more people are able to get medical help without worrying about money," "I agree with this statement. It keeps a limit on immigrants coming in and decreases acts of terrorism," "I know there are a lot of uninsured people still. This act did not fix the healthcare issue by far."
   - Causes: "I think President Trump had more people working, so not as many needed food stamps," "yes and it is the leaders that made the

dumb decisions that have made this happen," "global warming is affecting them."
4. **Rationalizing**
   – Bolstering: "I think that this is true from what I know about the Medicare system," "I believe this statement is true based on increased federal spending," "I think this is good, welfare is to help you get back on your feet and isn't something for life."
   – Denigrating: "This statement is based only on statistics," "The number may have decreased, but at cost to whom?" "If there is a time limit it doesn't seem to be enforced," "not enough policy to end to freeloaders."

In total, 63% (1,143) of respondents completed the open-ended question, and they were equally likely to respond to the policy-current and policy-outcome information. Of that 63%, 77% included content that fell into at least one of the four categories outlined above.[2] Table 5.3 shows the percent of respondents giving each type of response in answer to either the policy-current or policy-outcome facts. The categories were not mutually exclusive—for example, someone who said "this is true and very unfortunate" would be coded as both "contestation: true" and "evaluation: negative." The third column shows the result of a two-tailed *t*-test for differences between respondents who received a policy-outcome versus a policy-current fact.

Table 5.3 Open-ended responses to policy-current vs. policy-outcome facts

	Policy-current	Policy-outcome	Difference
Evaluation			
Positive	23%	8%	$t(7.2), p < .001$
Negative	6%	9%	$t(-1.8), p = .07$
Contestation			
False	7%	12%	$t(-3.1), p = .002$
True	18%	26%	$t(-3.5), p = .001$
Causal inference			
Effects	8%	5%	$t(2.1), p = .04$
Causes	6%	20%	$t(-7.0), p < .001$
Rationalizing			
Bolstering	12%	8%	$t(2.0), p = .04$
Denigrating	11%	10%	$t(0.6), p = .51$

Table 5.3 shows several systematic differences in how people respond to policy-current versus policy-outcome information. First, participants were much more positive about policy-current information than policy-outcome information. Indeed, some form of positive evaluation (e.g., "this is good") was the modal response to policy-current information.

Second, respondents were more likely to offer both "true" and "false" evaluations of policy-outcome statements than of policy-current statements. In total, 38% of responses to policy-outcome facts fell into one of these two categories, compared to 25% of policy-current responses. This pattern suggests that people perceive policy-outcome facts are inherently more *contestable* than policy-current facts.

People were slightly more likely to mention the potential effects of policy-current information and substantially more likely to make inferences about the *causes* of the policy-outcome information. Indeed, inferences about what might have caused a particular outcome comprised the second-most common response type to policy-outcome information.

Finally, there were only small differences between policy-outcome and policy-current facts in regards to bolstering and denigrating. Respondents were slightly more likely to engage in bolstering around policy-current facts (which makes some sense given that they also expressed more positive sentiment about these facts) and equally likely to engage in denigrating.

Study 1 discussion: How people interpret policy information

I began this chapter with a puzzle, asking why it was that giving people information about the outcomes of policies often seems to have minimal effects on their attitudes toward those policies, while giving them information about existing policies has a larger impact. I offered an initial explanation: people interpret policy-outcome information through a partisan lens and thus primarily use it to reinforce existing attitudes.

This study is an attempt to empirically test the first part of that explanation. First, I systematically compare how people react to policy-current versus policy-outcome information in ten different issue areas, and I find that they do indeed see policy-outcome information as more partisan. Then, I explore potential reasons for this difference by using open-ended questions to probe the specific interpretations and reactions that people have to policy-current versus policy-outcome information.

I find that there are three major differences in how people respond to policy-outcome versus policy-current information. Below I describe each of these in turn, first explaining why these differences might arise, and then discussing how they might contribute to differences in partisan interpretation (or the lack thereof).

Evaluation

Overall, respondents were far more likely to offer positive responses to policy-current information than to policy-outcome information. This tendency to approve of existing policy could be driven by the fact that policies (especially ones enacted prior to the current era of political polarization) are usually a product of at least some bipartisan compromise. For both the full set of issue areas, as well as within each individual issue area, Democrats and Republicans were equally likely to offer positive statements. For example, in response to learning that background checks are required for refugees entering the United States, a Democrat answered, "I agree with the policy and believe it should remain," while a Republican answered, "I completely agree."

Contestation

Facts about existing policy are descriptions of relatively concrete phenomena like laws and regulations. Facts about policy outcomes, however, require several levels of abstraction and reasoning, thus making them more open to critique—especially since there are usually multiple valid approaches to assess policy effects. For example, the effectiveness of the Affordable Care Act (ACA) could plausibly be measured via the change in the percentage of people who are insured, satisfaction with healthcare, or health outcomes (e.g., longevity). Then, there is the measurement itself: Did our measure actually capture the quantity of interest or was it biased in some way? Finally, there is the problem of making a causal connection between the establishment of a particular policy and its effects. As Bisgaard (2015, 851) points out, "In politics, judging who is responsible for a given outcome is inherently difficult." Given that social scientists consistently struggle to make these causal inferences, it should be unsurprising (and perhaps encouraging!) that everyday people are also skeptical of assuming a causal connection between a policy and an outcome.

While the majority of people who questioned the truth value of policy-outcome statements simply wrote responses like "Not true" or "It's wrong," many also offered critiques that explicitly mentioned the issues outlined above. For example, in response to learning that the crime rate among immigrants is lower than the crime rate among U.S. citizens, one person replied, "I think that it is false. Or biased as crime among immigrants are mostly unregistered."

Fundamentally, respondents are *right* to see facts about outcomes as more contestable than facts about existing policy. The fact that so many participants addressed the truth value of these outcome statements suggests that they are attuned to the practical difficulties of making accurate inferences about effects. They may not all have read the canonic book *How to Lie With Statistics*, but they have an intuitive sense that it can be done. Outcome facts are easier to counterargue, including in ways that are consistent with partisan predispositions.

Causal inference

We are wired to look for causal relationships: the human mind is "a machine for jumping to conclusions" Kahneman (2011). When people encounter a new piece of information they automatically make inferences about how that piece of information affects and is affected by other things in the world. The open-ended responses suggest that the nature of those inferences differ depending on the information. Twenty percent of responses to policy-outcome information included inferences about what *caused* that outcome (in contrast, only 6% of responses to policy-current information made inferences about what caused the policy). For example, in response to learning that Black children were more likely to attend a high-poverty school, one respondent said, "Blacks are certainly more impoverished than whites, and that inequality manifests in many ways, including school availability." In response to the fact that the percentage of food stamp recipients has declined since 2016, a respondent answered, "I believe, due to unemployment being lower during the Trump administration, more people were working and ineligible for food stamps."

Two phenomena are particularly relevant for understanding why people might be more likely to make partisan-influenced inferences about policy-outcome information: causal asymmetry, and the "explaining away" phenomenon. "Causal asymmetry" is the tendency for people to pay more attention and attribute more importance to the object or actor they perceive as *causal* in a given interaction. When considering a cause-effect relationship, people tend to "overestimate the strength or importance of the cause object and to underestimate or altogether neglect that of the effect object"

(White 2006, 142). The phenomenon of causal asymmetry suggests that when people are given a piece of information they conceptualize as an *effect* (e.g., the ball moved, the economy worsened), they will tend to infer a potential cause of that effect (a push, a policy) and then focus their cognitive attention on that cause. But if they are given a piece of information they interpret as a *cause* (e.g., a hurricane hit the coast, tax cuts were enacted), they may infer the *effects* of that cause but will still focus their attention on the initial cause.[3] Thus, policy-current information (a "cause") could spur people to consider the policy itself, while policy-outcome information (an "effect") could spur people to consider potential causes for that outcome.

The second relevant phenomenon occurs whenever people engage in cause-to-effect reasoning, which is called "explaining away." Explaining away occurs when a particular effect (or outcome) has multiple plausible causes. Given a particular effect, if we know that one of the potential causes definitely occurred, we perceive that the probabilities of the other causes go down, because no other causes are necessary (Rehder and Waldmann 2017; Sloman and Lagnado 2015). For any particular policy outcome (e.g., a decrease in unemployment during President Trump's first term), there are multiple potential causes. President Trump's tax cuts may have spurred businesses to hire, the economic reforms of the Obama administration may have finally borne fruit, or the global economy may have shifted to favor the United States. Of course, these varying explanations will not be equally accessible to everyone. A Democrat may know quite a bit about President Obama's reforms, and so that explanation is easy to retrieve, and the act of retrieving it makes others less plausible. A Republican, meanwhile, will find it easier to recall what Donald Trump has done, thereby rendering other explanations less likely.

Taken together, causal asymmetry and explaining away suggest a reason why partisanship could be more likely to influence interpretations of outcome facts. Causal asymmetry means that people focus on the *causal* part of a cause-effect pair. Thus, when given a policy outcome, people engage in the cognitive work to infer a cause, and the most accessible causes are likely those that reinforce their partisan predispositions.

Study 1 discussion

This chapter started out with a puzzle: Why is it that giving people relevant information about the outcomes of policies (i.e., "performance" measures) only rarely changes their attitudes? Building on existing work, I hypothesized that outcome information is especially subject to partisan interpretation, and that interpretation mutes its effects on opinions (Gaines et al. 2007). Study 1 tested this "partisan interpretation" hypothesis by directly comparing the perceived partisanship of policy-outcome versus policy-current facts. Across a wide range of issues, people rated the outcome statements as more likely to have been made by a partisan actor.

Study 1 also used an open-ended question to investigate how people respond to and interpret factual information. There were several systematic differences. Most notably, people were more positive toward information about existing policy, less likely to question its truth value, and less likely to make causal inferences.

However, Study 1 only solves one piece of the puzzle. We care about the extent to which partisanship informs interpretation because we suspect that when people interpret information through a partisan lens, those facts will then be used to reinforce rather than change attitudes. But is this really the case? The next section presents the results of a study designed to directly test the attitudinal impact of policy-outcome facts versus policy-current facts.

Study 2: Attitudinal effects of policy facts

This study, conducted with Lamis Abdelaaty, directly tests the hypothesis that policy-current information has a larger affect on attitudes than policy-outcome information.[4] In contrast to Study 1, which tested the impact of factual information across a range of issues, Study 2 focuses on one issue in particular: refugee policy. Refugee policy is a deliberately hard test of the hypothesis. It is fairly politicized: the results of Study 1 showed it was one of the issue areas with the least difference in partisan interpretation between policy-outcome and policy-current information. It is also a fairly salient issue, and one for which we might expect attitudes to be relatively stable.

Study 2 design

The survey experiment was fielded by Lucid in December 2020. In total, 2,565 people completed the survey, and all were included in the analyses. First, all respondents answered several demographic questions, including education, party identification, and whether one or both parents were born outside the U.S. All of these were asked prior to the treatment so they could be used as covariates in the experimental analyses.

Participants were then assigned to one of five conditions in a 2 (questions only vs. questions followed by corrective information) × 2 (policy-outcome vs. policy-current) plus control experiment. The full experimental design is illustrated in Figure 5.3.

Respondents in the "current refugee policy" conditions were asked four questions about existing refugee policy. The first question asked them to indicate what reasons qualify someone for refugee status (e.g., persecution for religious beliefs and coming from a country with high levels of corruption). The next three asked about refugee admission policy: whether refugees were required to undergo background checks, whether they received resettlement assistance, and whether they applied directly to the U.S. or to the U.N. Then, half were randomly assigned to see the correct answers to those policy questions.

Respondents in the "refugee policy outcomes" condition were asked questions about the *outcomes* of refugee policy: specifically, to estimate the size of the refugee population living in the United States, the percent convicted for terrorism-related offenses, and the percent dependent on welfare. These questions were based on similar measures used in past corrective interventions aimed at correcting misperceptions about immigrants (Hopkins et al. 2019; Jørgensen and Osmundsen 2022). Again, half were then randomly assigned to see the correct answers to these factual questions.

Respondents in a pure control condition saw neither set of questions, nor the answers. The inclusion of a pure control condition is necessary

	Refugee policy outcomes	Current refugee policy	
Questions only	• What proportion of U.S. residents are refugees • What proportion of refugees receive welfare benefits • What proportion of refugees have been convicted of terrorism-related offenses	• Reasons that qualify someone for refugee status (check all that apply) • Whether background checks are required • Whether refugees receive assistance • Whether refugees apply directly to U.S.	**Pure control** No questions or corrective information
Questions followed by corrective information	• Proportion of U.S. residents who are refugees (.06%) • Proportion of refugees who receive welfare benefits (6%) • Proportion of refugees who have been convicted of terrorism-related offenses (.00074%)	• Legal definition of refugees • Description of refugee application process • Description of refugee resettlement process	

Figure 5.3 Study 2 design

for establishing a baseline because the factual questions themselves (even without the information) may shape attitudes by making particular considerations (e.g., background checks or crime rates) more salient.

Next, all respondents answered a number of questions assessing their attitudes toward refugees. They indicated whether they supported or opposed five policies (1–5 scale, $M = 2.8$, $\alpha = .74$): giving loans to refugees to finance their travel to the U.S., allowing refugees to receive food stamps, allowing them to bring their immediate family members to the U.S., implementing stricter background checks, and temporarily pausing all refugee admissions during the COVID-19 pandemic. They were also shown images and brief biographic information about three refugees and asked whether they would support admitting them to the United States (1–5 scale, $M = 3.8$, $\alpha = .74$).

Study 2 results

At the end of the survey, respondents were asked slightly different versions of the same factual questions that they were asked earlier. These questions served as a manipulation check. In the "existing refugee policy" condition, respondents who received the corrective information answered 4.8 of the seven questions correctly, compared to 3.7 among those who did not ($T = -7.3$, $p<.001$). In the "refugee policy outcomes" condition, respondents who received the corrective information answered 1.2 out of the three questions correctly, compared to .7 for those who did not ($T = -8.9$, $p<.001$). The results suggest that both treatments were successful at changing factual beliefs.

Prevalence of misperceptions

In the "policy outcomes" condition, the median number of questions correct was two out of three, and in the "existing policy" condition, the median number was four out of six.[5] Thus, the modal respondent in both groups answered at least 50% of the questions correctly, suggesting that both types of misperceptions are prevalent but not omnipresent.

Table 5.4 shows the most commonly held misperceptions about existing refugee policy. Almost two-thirds of respondents believed that refugees apply directly to the U.S. government rather than to the U.N. and that coming from a country with high levels of crime, poverty, or corruption qualifies a person

Table 5.4 Commonly held misperceptions about existing refugee policy

	Percent
Refugees apply directly to the U.S. government	60%
Coming from a poor/corrupt/high-crime country qualifies someone for refugee status	58%
No background checks are required for refugees	32%
Refugees receive no resettlement assistance	25%
Having little skills/education qualifies someone for refugee status	24%

for refugee status. More than one in four respondents believed that no background checks are required for refugees.

Misperceptions about policy outcomes were also widespread. Similar to previous surveys measuring misperceptions about immigrants, respondents in the "outcomes" condition substantially overestimated the prevalence of refugees (median answer = 19%, correct answer = .06%), their dependence on welfare (median answer = 19%, correct answer = 6%), and their rate of terrorism-related convictions (median answer = 5%, correct answer = .00074%).

Effects of policy-current vs. policy-outcome information on attitudes
Figure 5.4 shows the effect of the treatments on support for refugee-friendly policies and willingness to admit specific refugees, as compared to the pure control condition. Partisanship, political interest, education, gender, race, and whether parents were immigrants are included as covariates in the models (results are consistent when covariates are omitted; see Thorson and Abdelaaty (2023)). Neither the questions nor corrective information about policy outcomes have a significant effect on policy support or support for admission.

Those who were asked questions about refugee admission without being given the correct answer were slightly more supportive of refugee-friendly policies than those in the control condition. In other words, simply making aspects of existing refugee policy salient increased support. This finding speaks to the importance of including a pure control condition in experimental designs testing the impact of corrective information (rather than simply using the "uncorrected" group as a control).

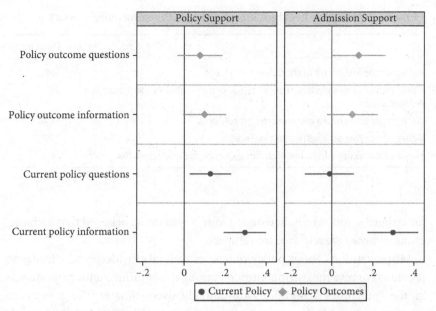

Figure 5.4 Effect of information about policy outcomes and existing policy on support for refugee-friendly policies (1-5 scale)

More importantly, receiving corrective information about the existing refugee admission process substantially increased support for refugee-friendly policies, moving respondents by about .3 on a 4-point scale. To put this effect size in context, it is a similar magnitude to the difference between Independents and Democrats. The positive effect of receiving information about current policy is not conditional on party.

Study 2 discussion

Misperceptions about refugees are widespread. People hold false beliefs about both existing refugee policy (e.g., what qualifies someone as a refugee) and about the outcomes of those policies (e.g., the percent of refugees who receive welfare benefits). While corrective information makes people more accurate across the board, only information about existing policy also has downstream effects on attitudes. Respondents who saw corrective information about existing policy were substantially more supportive of refugee-friendly policies than those who saw corrective information about policy outcomes. These results of Study 1 are consistent with the partisan rationalization hypothesis: people accepted the policy-outcome information but did not use it to update their attitudes, potentially because they engaged in partisan interpretation of this information.

Conclusion

Widespread misperceptions are a concern because they have the potential to distort attitudes. However, an association between a misperception and an attitude (e.g., a belief in death panels and dislike of the ACA) does not guarantee that there is a causal link between the two. The only way of establishing that causal link is through experiments that directly test how exposure to misinformation (or, more ethically, corrections) shapes attitudes. This chapter begins by reviewing a set of studies that do just that, using experiments to examine the downstream effects of policy information on policy attitudes. The results reveal a surprising pattern: across a range of studies, corrective information about the *outcomes* of policies has a minimal effect on attitudes.

I argue that information about outcomes invites a type of interpretation that opens the door for partisan considerations. As Porter and Wood (2019, 72) put it: "Political attitudes, particularly when they are enmeshed in partisanship and the presidency, have best a distant relationship to facts." Evidence from Study 1, which included both a survey and an open-ended question, supports the hypothesis that policy-outcome information is indeed "enmeshed in partisanship." Across a range of issues, people see information about policy outcomes as more partisan than information about existing policy.

Study 2 directly compared the attitudinal effects of exposure to corrective information about existing policy versus policy outcomes in a specific issue area. Correcting misperceptions about existing policy had a strong and significant effect on attitudes about refugees, while correcting misperceptions about policy outcomes had no effect. However, this study only compared the attitudinal effects of policy-outcome versus policy-current information in a single-issue area. In Chapter 6 I examine how policy-current information affects attitudes across four issue domains: Social Security, TANF, refugee policy, and the national debt.

6
Policy misperceptions and competence

Chapter 5 investigated how partisanship might color interpretation of policy information, arguing that corrective information about existing policy may be particularly likely to change downstream attitudes because it is less subject to partisan interpretation. Study 2 in Chapter 5 offered initial support for that hypothesis: people who were given information about existing refugee policy were substantially more supportive of refugee policies than those in a control group. In contrast, providing information about policy *outcomes* had no effect on policy opinions. However, this study had two major limitations: it examined the impact of policy-current information in a single area (refugee policy) and on a single type of opinion (policy support). This chapter presents the results of a study designed to systematically assess the effects of exposure to corrective information about existing policy across a range of issues and for a range of opinions.

Specifically, I test the effect of corrective information on two attitudinal outcomes: *policy approval*, or the extent to which people approve of existing policy; and *policy priorities*, or the specific aspects of the policy they want to keep and/or change. I predict that policy misperceptions will decrease approval of existing policy (and conversely, correcting those misperceptions will increase approval). As described in previous chapters, political actors often deliberately critique standing policy. By increasing public dissatisfaction with the status quo, they can more easily build support for their own policies. For example, politicians' misleading rhetoric about Social Security directly shaped the public's factual beliefs about the issue in ways that increased concern about the program's future (Jerit and Barabas 2006).

In addition, misperceptions about existing policy can distort policy priorities, which I operationalize as the specific aspects of a policy that a person wants to retain or change. Policy misperceptions can affect priorities because a person's opinions about what the government *should* do are shaped partly by what they think the government is *currently* doing. For example, the misperception that there is no time limit on TANF benefits might lead a person to support adding means testing and other restrictions on who can receive assistance. Alternatively, the misperception that the U.S. spends more on military than on healthcare might lead them to prioritize substantially reducing military spending. Policy misperceptions will shape priorities in different ways depending on the issue area, the individual, and the misperception. The goal of this chapter is not to show that correcting policy misperceptions has always has the same effect across issue areas; rather, it is to illustrate the myriad of ways in which learning about current policy can reshape priorities.

Study 1: How policy-current information shapes beliefs and opinions

This study tests the effect of corrective policy-current information on policy approval and priorities by randomly assigning participants to read news articles containing concise descriptions of existing policy. The experiment is designed to increase external validity by presenting respondents with a treatment similar to how they might encounter policy-current information in the real world (given, of course, the constraints of an experimental setting) (Druckman 2022). In most other experiments in this book, the correct information is embedded in the experiment without a specific source provided. For example, in the refugee study in Chapter 5, respondents were given a short text blurb with accurate information about the refugee admission process. But in the real world, most people likely encounter policy-current information in the context of a news article, with all the attendant biases and skepticism.

Also, unlike other experiments in this book (and many other experiments that employ corrective interventions), I do not ask any factual questions prior to the information treatment. This choice likely reduces the magnitude of effects. As Kuklinski et al. (2000, 805) point out, corrective information is most effective at changing attitudes when "presented in a way that 'hits them between the eyes' by drawing attention to its policy relevance and explicitly correcting misperceptions." In their study, they find that corrective information about welfare has the largest attitudinal effects when they ask participants what they think welfare spending should be and what they think it actually is, then point out that the real number is much closer to their ideal estimate than they believed. Similarly, the refugee study in Chapter 5 first asks people factual questions about refugees, then provides them the correct answer.

While this ask-then-correct strategy is useful for identifying causal effects, it is also unlikely to occur in the real world. Normally, people encounter information without having first been asked explicit questions about it, and the goal of this chapter and the next is to evaluate not only how interventions to dismantle the invented state might work in theory, but also how they could be implemented at a practical level. Thus, the experiments in this chapter are a "harder test" in which people are not "hit between the eyes" with the discrepancy between their beliefs and the facts; rather, they are presented with factual information in a format and style that is very similar to how they might encounter it in the real world.

Study design

Respondents (N = 3,878) were recruited via the survey platform Lucid. They first answered several demographic questions, including their age and political interest. They were then randomly assigned to one of four policy areas: refugee policy, Social Security, TANF, or the national debt. These policy areas were selected because each includes a range of policy-current misperceptions identified by previous research in this book. However, they also vary along a number of dimensions, including the extent to which they are associated with partisan identity and the extent to which they affect participants directly.

Within each policy area, the treatment group read a news article that gave information about existing policy. The control group proceeded directly to the dependent variables (which were specific to each policy). Thus, the study consisted of four separate "mini-experiments," each of which had a unique (though structurally parallel) set of dependent variables.

Although the treatment articles contained policy-specific information, they were written to be similar in format as possible. Each was about 200 words long and had the headline "Key Facts About [Policy]." The articles were formatted to look as much as possible like "real" news articles and provided simple background information about each policy. Participants were told that the article was a feature from a local newspaper. Below is the text for the article describing Social Security policy. The articles on refugee policy, TANF, and the national debt followed a similar format.

Key Facts About the Social Security Program
Social Security is a government program designed to help provide a financial safety net for retired people, disabled people, and their families. The Social Security program was signed into law in 1935.
How is Social Security funded?
Social Security is funded by taxes on people who are currently employed. Employees and employers both pay 6.2% of their wages into the Social Security Trust Fund. This means that if Sam makes $30,000 a year working at Costco, then he and Costco each pay about $78 per month into the Fund. The money from Sam and his employer, along with millions of other workers and their employers, pays for Social Security benefits.
Who can receive Social Security benefits?
Most Social Security benefits go to retired people and their families. Retirees can start receiving benefits at age 62 but receive more if they retire later (up to age 67), and 97% of elderly Americans receive Social Security benefits. The longer a person works, the more benefits they receive upon retirement. A small portion of benefits go to people with long-term disabilities, including those they received while working. The average Social Security retirement benefit is about $1,514 per month, and disabled workers receive slightly less.

Participants in the four treatment conditions proceeded to the dependent variables after reading the article, while those in the control conditions answered the dependent variable questions immediately after answering the demographic questions. The following sections describe the three dependent variables (misperceptions, policy approval, and policy priorities) in more detail.

Misperceptions

Measuring misperceptions post-treatment makes it possible to test whether exposure to the article reduces policy misperceptions. For each policy area, I ask three factual questions designed to tap common misperceptions, using the same dichotomous format used throughout the book ("Which of these statements is correct? If you're not sure, please give your best guess"). The correct answers to all three of the questions are included in the relevant articles. Table 6.1 shows which misperceptions are measured for each issue area.

Approval of existing policy

I measure policy approval with three 5-point agree-disagree questions: "The U.S. should substantially change [policy]," "Reforming [policy] should be a top priority for Congress," "The current [policy] works well," and one 5-point approve/disapprove question ("Do you approve or disapprove of existing [policy]?") This measure is designed to capture satisfaction with existing policy. I hypothesize that reading the corrective information will *increase* approval for all four policies.

Policy priorities

Each respondent answered two open-ended questions about the specific policy they were assigned to. Similar to other studies in this book, I use open-ended questions to produce a measure that does not presume how corrective information "should" change opinions. Specifically, I ask respondent to indicate one thing they would *change* about the policy, and one thing they would *keep the same* about the policy. While these outcomes (unlike "satisfaction with existing policy") have the disadvantage of not being directly comparable across studies, they do allow me to explore systematic differences between the priorities expressed by respondents in the treatment versus control conditions within each issue.

The open-ended responses were coded inductively. In each category, I read a sample of 100 responses and used that sample to generate the categories for the rest of the responses. Four categories were the same across all issue areas: non-response (any blank or non-substantive response), "nothing" (implying that nothing should change and/or stay the same about the policy), "other" (any specific policy recommendation that was made by fewer than 20 respondents), and "don't know."

Table 6.2 shows the additional categories created for each issue area. A response was given a "1" if it fell into each category and a "0" otherwise. Although the categories were not mutually exclusive, the substantial majority of responses fell into only one category (likely because the question specifically asked respondents to mention "one thing they would change" and "one thing they would keep the same").

Table 6.1 Misperceptions measured by issue area

Issue area	Correct answer	Incorrect answer
National debt	China holds less than half of U.S. debt.	China holds more than half of U.S. debt.
	Interest on the federal debt is less than half of federal spending.	Interest on the federal debt is more than half of federal spending.
	Most interest payments on the national debt go to American investors who have bought U.S. Treasury bonds, bills, and notes.	Most interest payments on the national debt go to foreign investors who have bought U.S. Treasury bonds, bills, and notes.
TANF	Currently, there is a federal limit on how long a person can receive welfare (TANF) benefits.	Currently, there is no federal limit on how long a person can receive welfare (TANF) benefits.
	Less than half of families living in poverty receive welfare (TANF) benefits.	More than half of families living in poverty receive welfare (TANF) benefits.
	Undocumented immigrants are not eligible to receive TANF (welfare) benefits.	Undocumented immigrants are eligible to receive TANF (welfare) benefits.
Social Security	Social Security benefits are paid for by taxes on people who are currently employed.	Social Security benefits are paid for by money that retired people contributed to their personal Social Security savings account while they were employed.
	Both employees and employers contribute money to the Social Security trust fund.	Only employees contribute money to the Social Security trust fund.
	Most Social Security benefits go to retired people.	Most Social Security benefits go to disabled people.
Refugees	Refugees are required to pass international and domestic background checks before being admitted to the United States.	Refugees are not required to pass international and domestic background checks before being admitted to the United States.
	People who live in countries with extreme poverty do not automatically qualify for refugee status.	People who live in countries with extreme poverty automatically qualify for refugee status.
	Refugees who wish to resettle in the United States must register with the United Nations before applying to the U.S. government.	Refugees who wish to resettle in the United States apply directly to the U.S. government.

Table 6.2 Policy priorities: Distribution of open-ended responses

	Priority to change	Frequency	Priority to keep	Frequency
Refugee policy	More entrance requirements	20.7% (203)	Admission process	21.1% (207)
	Fewer entrance requirements	14.1% (138)	Eligibility criteria	5.4% (53)
Social Security	Protection from govt	5.4% (53)	Age requirements	7.7% (75)
	Restrict benefits	6.2% (60)	Funding structure	8.9% (87)
	Expand benefits	21.9% (213)	Beneficiaries	11.3% (110)
TANF	Restrict benefits	17.9% (174)	Eligibility criteria	10.9% (106)
	Expand benefits	15.4% (149)	Time limits	4.6% (45)
	Benefit distribution	2.4% (23)	Nature of benefits	17.8% (173)
National debt	Cut spending	14.6% (139)	Debt reduction	4.2% (40)
	Force a balanced budget	5.7% (54)	Avoid spending cuts	11.0% (105)
	Raise taxes	7.6% (73)	Debt structure	7.0% (67)

The following section details specific examples of answers that fell into each of the 22 substantive categories, along with examples of answers that were categorized as "other."

Refugee policy: Priority to change
More entrance requirements: This category encompasses any recommendation to make entrance requirements for refugees stricter. For example, "Vet applicants thoroughly and only ones that enter the country at the legal ports of entry," "They need to register before accepting them," and "more background checks."

Fewer entrance requirements: This category encompasses any recommendation that would make it easier for refugees to enter the United States. For example, "We should increase the number of situations that qualify for refugee status," "They can bring as much immediate family as long as they check out," and "make the legal system easier for them to work with and have a shorter time for the processing."

Other: This category includes responses that are substantive and related to the prompt, but it is unclear whether the respondent was advocating policies that were more or less strict. For example, "the process," "the number itself," and "the method of checking backgrounds."

Refugees: Priority to keep
Admission process: This category includes responses that describe the existing admission process. For example, "vetting them and background checks," "the government review process," "registering with the UN," and "background checks."

Eligibility criteria: This category includes responses that describe the types of people who qualify for refugee status. For example, "Prioritize refugees on the basis of need for asylum or admission on humanitarian grounds," "Allow those facing persecution," "Allow immigrants from war torn countries."

Other: This category includes any substantive responses that did not fall into the other two categories. For example, "Trying to honor human rights during the process," "Transparency," and "That all USA policies are strictly followed."

Social Security: Priority to change
Protection from government: This category includes responses that advocate preventing the government from using Social Security funds for other purposes, for example "keep government hands off it," "stop using it for national debt," "stop using it for other things," and "Make it so that politicians can't keep borrowing for their pork barrel interests and depleting the trust fund."

Restrict benefits: This category includes responses that suggest benefits should be restricted in some way: for example, "work restrictions," "Too much disability for people able to work," "too many unqualified receiving ssi benefits," "That illegal immigrants shouldn't receive Social Security," and "stop giving benefits to people who did not pay into the system."

Expand benefits: Responses in these categories advocated expanding benefits and/or making them easier to access. For example, "To make it accessible to all," "to help poor people," "There should be an increase because $900 a month is not enough for someone to survive in today's day and age," "social security should be available to more disabled people also," and "More money to senior citizens."

Other: This category includes substantive responses that did not fall into the other categories, for example, "More staff to reduce backlog of cases and be more responsive to calls," "make the application process simpler," and "make all benefits nontaxable."

Social Security: What would you keep the same?
Age requirements: These responses specifically mentioned the age requirements for Social Security, for example "retirement age of 65," "keep ages of eligibility in place," "I would keep the age of retirement the same," and "age criteria."

Funding structure: Responses in this category referenced how Social Security is funded, for example, "You get what you put back when you retire," "worker/employer contributions," "to keep it taxpayer and employer funded," "That people earn it by working and they put it aside towards their retirement," "keep it funded by taxes," and "how it's funded."

Beneficiaries: These responses discussed who receives Social Security benefits, for example, "who the funds go to," "who is legally eligible to receive it," "The fact that it goes to help disabled and retired people," "giving to the old."

Other: This category includes substantive responses that did not fall into the other categories, for example "website," "the option to delay taking it," "have a safety net," "direct deposit."

TANF: What would you change?
Restrict benefits: Responses in this category proposed restricting who receives benefits and/or making them more difficult to access. For example, "Where people can spend the money . . . not on hair products . . . only for food and medicine," "Who get food support. Too many people get food stamps that don't need them," "That adults responsible for applying whether for themselves or their children should have to prove they are looking for work," "require random drug testing to qualify," "If you become pregnant while on the program, you can't get additional benefits."

Expand benefits: Responses in this category proposed expanding who receives benefits and/or making existing benefits more accessible. For example, "Who can qualify. People without children need help too," "make it more accessible," "time limit increase," "They should increase the amount of money families receive because sometime the amount of money that certain families get is not enough got them," "Reevaluate the program's qualifications so more families are eligible," "more money to help people."

Benefit distribution: These responses advocated changing how benefits are distributed. For example, "That states can decide the amount of cash disbursements. It should be based on the cost of living in the state with at least a minimum base payment," "should be more standardized as to state to state percentages that are used for cash allocations."

Other: This category includes substantive responses that did not fall into the other categories (e.g., "The attitude with the staff") as well as suggestions that could plausibly refer to either expanding or restricting benefits (e.g., "Who is eligible," "the amount received").

TANF: What would you keep the same?
Eligibility criteria: This category refers to statements about wanting to keep some aspect of the eligibility requirements for TANF. For example, "That funds go to families with children 18 and under," "That no illegal aliens can benefit from it," "the age requirements," "only for legal citizens," "I would keep that if you make under a certain amount you qualify for the benefits."

Time limits: Responses in this category mention the TANF time limit. For example, "The 2 year limit," "I would keep the eligibility years [2] same," "duration," "A person can only receive benefits for 2 consecutive years," and "2 year max."

Nature of benefits: These responses mentioned the benefits that TANF provides. For example, "The amount of money the family receives," "the benefit amount per child," "provide families with financial aid," "it provides appropriate benefit amounts," "I would keep the monetary benefits the same," and "cash benefits"

Other: Responses in this category include substantive answers that did not fall into other categories, such as "keeping it a monthly payment" and "congressional oversite."

National debt policy: What would you change?
Cut spending: These responses suggested specific areas to cut to reduce the national debt, for example, "Take money from social programs to repay the debt," "stop wasteful spending," "stop giving money to red states," "pay cut for congress and the senate," and "I would reduce military expenses"

Force a balanced budget: Responses in this category advocated eliminating the ability to raise the debt ceiling and/or enforce a balanced budget. For example, "The debt ceiling can not be constantly raised," "the ability to raise the limit," "Seems like there should be a certain percentage beyond which the debt ceiling cannot be raised," "force a balanced budget amendment so that if you want a new program, you have to raise revenue to pay for it fully."

Raise taxes: Responses in this category suggested raising taxes (usually, though not always, on the wealthy) to reduce the debt. For example, "the elite rich to pay higher taxes and stop the evading paying anything at all as most of the do," "tax rich people more," and "Raise taxes on the wealthy to reduce debt."

Other: This category includes substantive responses that did not fall into the other categories, such as "The amount of money paid to Congress and the amount of inside trading done by that body of government," "Make students pay back government loans they got in college," "strong effort to reduce it," "pay it up quickly," "make sure money is spent equally," and "Having congress require a super majority vote."

National debt policy: What would you keep the same?
Debt reduction efforts: Responses in this category supported continued efforts to reduce the debt. For example, "stop additional spending," "reduce unnecessary items," "cut unnecessary spending."

Avoid spending cuts: These responses specifically mentioned a government-run program that should not be cut to reduce the national debt, for example, "The amount of money allotted for social security," "Support programs for the United States citizens that need them," and "spending for social programs."

Debt structure: This category includes mentions of how U.S. debt is structured. For example, "The amount of return to Americans," "That most of the treasury stocks are owned by Americans," "Majority owed to Americans," "Keep money being paid to the citizenry through treasury bonds," and "I would continue to allow citizens to invest thru treasury bills."

Other: This category includes substantive responses that did not fall into the other categories, such as "The rules of the policy," "The way they handle business," "the people who need it and get help," "issuing pre-paid cards for people with lower credit scores," and "the coronavirus."

Results: How corrective information about existing policy affects beliefs and attitudes

The experiment explored how providing accurate information about existing policy affected three separate dependent variables: accuracy, approval of existing policy, and policy priorities.

Accuracy

All participants answered three questions about the policy area to which they were assigned. As in previous studies, the question format provided respondents with two different statements and asked them to choose the correct one. (The full text of these statements is in Table 6.1.) Correct responses were added together to form a 0–3 scale. Looking only at the control condition within each issue area, people were most accurate on Social Security ($M = 2.1$, $SE = .04$), followed by refugee policy ($M = 1.8$, $SE = .04$) and TANF ($M = 1.5$, $SE = .05$). They were least accurate on debt, answering an average of just 1.1 out of the three questions correctly ($SE = .05$). Figure 6.1 shows the overall effect of the treatment on accuracy, controlling for individual issue areas (with Social Security as the reference category for issues).

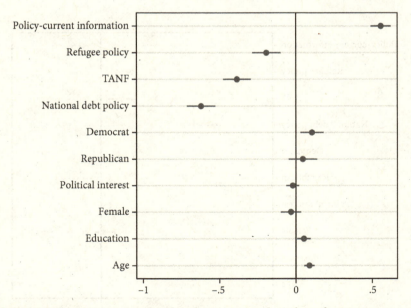

Figure 6.1 Factors associated with policy accuracy (number of correct answers, 0–3 scale)

For every issue, reading the article significantly decreased misperceptions. Unsurprisingly, given that people held the most misperceptions about the national debt, the corrective intervention made the biggest difference in increasing accuracy (from 1.1 questions correct in the control group to 2.1 in the treatment condition). More-educated people were more accurate on Social Security and the national debt, but not TANF or refugee policy. Partisan identity was a predictor only for TANF, where Democrats were more accurate than Independents. And finally, age was positively associated with accuracy on Social Security.

Policy approval

Policy approval was measured with an index of four questions (1–5 scale).[1] In the control group, people were most satisfied with Social Security policy (M = 2.8, SE = .04), followed by TANF (M = 2.7, SE = .04), refugee policy (M = 2.6, SE = .04), and finally national debt policy (M = 2.2, SE = .04). Figure 6.2 shows the results of a regression predicting policy approval across all four issues, controlling for individual issue areas (with Social Security as the reference category for issues).

Policy-current information has a small but significant positive effect on policy approval. Across the four issue areas, respondents who read the policy

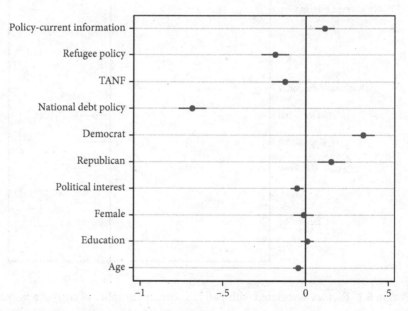

Figure 6.2 Factors associated with policy approval (1-5 scale)

information move about .1 on a 1–5 approval scale. Both Democrats and Republicans are more likely to approve of existing policy than Independents, and political interest and age are both negatively associated with approval.

Policy priorities

The analyses in this section all use the responses to the two open-ended questions asked at the end of the survey: "What is one thing you would change about [policy]?" and "What is one thing you would keep the same about [policy]?"

First, I examine a category that is comparable across both questions and all four issues: non-response.[2] Figure 6.3 shows the effect of the policy-current information on non-response for both the "change" and "same" questions. Exposure to the corrective information significantly decreases non-response to both the questions: "What would you keep the same about [policy]" and "What would you change about [policy]."

Next, I compare how exposure to corrective information about existing policy changes participants' priorities within each individual policy area. Table 6.3 shows the percentage of responses to "What is one thing you would change about [policy]?" in the treatment and control condition that fell into

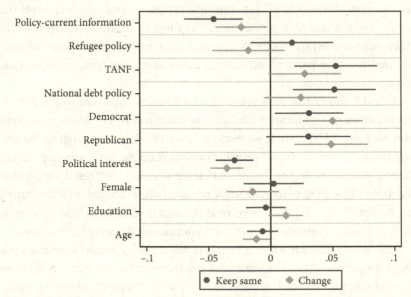

Figure 6.3 Factors associated with non-response to "What would you keep the same/change about [policy]

112 THE INVENTED STATE

Table 6.3 Priorities to change (open-ended)

	Control	Treatment	Significant?
TANF			
Expand benefits	16%	15%	
Restrict benefits	17%	19%	
Benefit distribution	1%	5%	√
Refugee policy			
More entrance requirements	23%	19%	√
Fewer entrance requirements	14%	14%	
Social Security			
Protection from govt	6%	5%	
Restrict benefits	7%	6%	
Expand benefits	19%	25%	√
National debt			
Cut spending	14%	16%	
Force a balanced budget	4%	7%	
Raise taxes	6%	9%	

each of the substantive categories. Note that the categories do not sum to 100 because responses could fall into multiple categories and non-responses and "other" are not included in the table. The third column shows whether the difference between treatment and control is significant in a regression analysis that includes party identification, political interest, gender, education, and age as covariates.

Table 6.3 shows that in three of the four issues, exposure to the corrective information significantly changed the pattern of responses. Respondents who read the TANF article were more likely to advocate changing the way benefits are distributed and decisions about funding are made (e.g., at the state vs. federal level). The refugee article significantly decreased the number of people advocating more restrictive refugee policy (consistent with Study 2 in Chapter 5). Finally, those who read the Social Security article were more likely to suggest expanding benefits and/or making them easier to access.

Table 6.4 shows that when it comes to what people would keep the same about the policies, the difference between treatment and control conditions is even more pronounced. Across the 11 separate categories, there is a significant difference between treatment and control in seven. It makes intuitive sense that the corrective information (which describes current policy) would

Table 6.4 Priorities to keep (open-ended)

	Control	Treatment	Significant?
TANF			
Eligibility criteria	8%	14%	√
Time limits	2%	8%	√
Nature of benefits	21%	15%	√
Refugee policy			
Admission process	17%	26%	√
Eligibility criteria	6%	4%	
Social Security			
Age requirements	8%	8%	
Funding structure	5%	12%	√
Beneficiaries	11%	12%	
National debt			
Debt reduction	14%	16%	√
Avoid spending cuts	4%	7%	
Debt structure	6%	9%	√

have an outsize impact on attitudes towards that policy. Many of the factors that people mentioned in the open-ended responses directly paralleled some of the content in the corrective information. For example, more than one in four people who read the refugee article (which included detailed information about how refugees enter the country) advocated keeping existing admission procedures, compared to just 17% of those who did not read the article. Taken together, Tables 6.3 and 6.4 show that exposure to the corrective information substantially changes how people think about these policies. However, it is important to treat these results as exploratory: they are not tests of hypotheses generated prior to the experiment, and they are not adjusted for multiple comparisons.

It is worth noting that in both categories responses discussing *program funding* were notably absent. Even though the questions explicitly asked what should be kept or changed about the policy, very few people mentioned levels of spending. Spending's absence from these responses is notable given that questions asking about program funding (e.g., "Should spending on [policy] be increased or decreased?") are one of the most common closed-ended formats for gauging policy opinions, partially because (unlike many other types of questions) it is easily kept consistent across issue types. While questions about preferred spending may be convenient for measurement purposes, these results suggest that they may not actually assess a particularly salient aspect of policy for most people.

Discussion

I find that exposure to corrective information about existing policy in the form of news articles has three effects. First, it is highly effective at reducing misperceptions across multiple issue areas. Second, it significantly increases approval of existing policies. And finally, it alters policy priorities, primarily by changing the specific aspects of policies that people feel strongly about keeping in place.

The use of open-ended questions to measure the effect of policy-current information on priorities does not neatly map onto how political scientists tend to conceptualize and measure public opinion. Typically, researchers measure policy attitudes with general questions tapping (for example) preferences for more or less spending. In contrast, the questions in this study ask people to articulate specific aspects of a given policy that they want to change and keep. This approach has clear drawbacks. First, because not all participants are equally likely to provide substantive responses to open-ended questions, it has the potential to introduce bias. Second, employing open-ended questions makes it more difficult to compare effect sizes across issues.

However, using open-ended questions also has several advantages. Most importantly, it allows for a more fine-grained measurement of how different considerations become more or less salient when shown information about existing policy. Measures of overall support or spending, while having the advantage of being comparable across issue areas, cannot provide much insight into what *aspects* of policy people support and/or oppose. In contrast, this study can tell us that (for example) people become substantially more supportive of expanding Social Security benefits when they learn how the program actually works. These fine-grained preferences may be more difficult to measure, but they are key to assessing democratic competence. They serve as a bridge between a person's underlying values and experience and their overall policy support (Mutz 1993).

Conclusion

It is important to note that that precisely how corrective information about existing policy shapes attitudes varies between and within policy area. For example, it leads more people to express support for keeping the current eligibility criteria for TANF benefits, but fewer to express support for maintaining the same *type* of benefits. People who learn more about Social Security are more confident in its funding structure, but equally likely to want to restrict benefits. Policies are complex, and people's attitudes towards those policies are not unidimensional.

The study described in this chapter cannot provide a definitive single answer to the question of how dismantling the invented state shapes opinions, both because there is no such single answer and because the study is exploratory rather than confirmatory. Rather, it suggests an alternative approach to understanding opinions about policy: an approach that acknowledges both the complexity of policy opinions and the role of factual beliefs (and misperceptions) in their construction. Across a range of issue areas, dismantling the invented state can have a powerful effect on downstream opinions. Exposure to corrective information about existing policy not only reduces misperceptions and increases support for existing policies, but it also alters priorities across a range of issues.

7
Dismantling the invented state

In his canonic 1922 book *Public Opinion*, Walter Lippmann argued that Americans react not to the political world as it is but to the simplistic "pictures in their head" that they have created of that world. Lippmann enlists the fictional Miss Sherwin of Gopher Prairie to illustrate his argument. He describes how Miss Sherwin, "aware that a war is raging in France," conceives of this war by creating a mental image "not unlike an Eighteenth Century engraving of a great soldier. He stands there boldly unruffled and more than life size, with a shadowy army of tiny little figures winding off into the landscape behind" (Lippmann 1922, 12–13). When I assign this chapter of *Public Opinion* to my students, someone invariably brings Miss Sherwin into our class discussion of the text. She is a powerful metaphor partly because she is so familiar. Miss Sherwin viscerally reminds us of our own experience trying to comprehend the complicated and often abstract world of politics.

What would the invented state look like rendered in Lippmann's prose? We could imagine Mr. Farley of San Jose, who imagines the Social Security program as an imposing neoclassical building. Each month his payments arrive and are deposited in a safety deposit box engraved with his name. But sometimes, a sinister government official intercepts the deposit, siphoning off some of Mr. Farley's hard-earned savings to pay for heated toilet seats in congressional bathrooms.

Our goal cannot and should not be to replace Mr. Farley's distorted mental image with a photo-realistic one. Reality, as Lippmann readily acknowledges, is too messy, too complicated, and most of all, too big for us to understand in its entirety. The pictures in our heads will always be approximations. Our goal, then, is not perfect realism, but rather to minimize the extent to which these pictures—and in particular the ones about policy—distort attitudes and behavior. We can design corrective interventions showing Mr. Farley that the money he deposits goes not to his own account but to help fund his parents' monthly checks, and we can help him visualize the alarms that have been set to protect against thieves.

In this chapter, I address two of the most common responses I (or anyone) receive when they propose an intervention that fundamentally amounts to informing people about public policy: first, that facts don't matter in politics, and second, that nobody cares about policy. Or, to put these two responses in more formal terms, that efforts at policy education will be thwarted by *resistance* and/or *indifference*.

Resistance occurs when a person fails to accept a correction, often due to partisan-driven motivated reasoning. A canonic example of resistance is many Republicans' steadfast refusal to accept that Barack Obama was born in the United States, despite the overwhelming evidence to the contrary. For these Republicans, the misperception is inextricably linked to their partisan identity. More recently, the same pattern has emerged around false claims of voter fraud during the 2020 election. Because these claims have been repeated and amplified by Republican elites (in particular, Donald Trump), they have become integral to Republican identity and are thus difficult to dislodge.

The flip side of resistance is indifference, that is, when a person cares so little about a topic that they fail to integrate or recall new information about it. If a person does not care about policy (be it Social Security or TANF), they may not bother with the cognitive work it takes to update their beliefs (Anderson 1981).

To sum up, a correction may fail to "stick" for two reasons: if a person refuses to accept it (often because it conflicts with an aspect of their identity), or if a person does not care enough to pay attention to (much less recall) the correction. In this chapter, I describe both phenomena in more detail, and I then empirically test how the effectiveness of policy corrections are affected by two factors: resistance (do people with ideological commitments resist policy corrections?) and indifference (do policy corrections fade over time?).

Why people may resist policy corrections

A popular narrative holds that people are not only resistant to corrections but also, in many cases, corrections backfire, leading people to double down on their incorrect beliefs. Paul Krugman, writing in the *New York Times*, proclaimed that "facts not only don't win arguments, they make people on the wrong side dig in even deeper." Krugman is incorrect. Substantial experimental research suggests that most corrections, even about polarizing political issues, are at least somewhat successful in increasing accuracy (Wood and Porter 2019) and the backfire effect is extremely rare (Nyhan 2021). Our default assumption, then, should be that corrective interventions make people, on average, more accurate. Still, this assumption is worth testing empirically, in part because most studies assessing the effectiveness of corrections have focused on political rather than policy misperceptions. This section outlines two potential (not mutually exclusive) reasons that people might not accept corrective interventions about existing policy: they may be reluctant to undermine their mental models, and they may be unwilling to accept corrections that run counter to their ideological commitments.

Resistance to dismantling mental models

As Chapter 4 shows, the misperceptions that make up the invented state often (though not always) originate partly from citizens' attempts to understand complex policy issues. It is possible that this inferential process makes policy misperceptions uniquely difficult to dislodge. Corrections can be less effective when a particular misperception plays a critical role in a person's mental model of an event or situation: "People prefer to have an inaccurate over an incomplete event model, which can lead to reliance upon discredited information even after an explicit correction" (Swire and Ecker 2018).

For example, imagine a person who heard a 2020 speech from then-President Donald Trump, proclaiming that refugees were "overwhelming public resources, overcrowding schools, and inundating your hospitals" (Shesgreen 2020). This person might infer (not illogically) that refugees are entering the country unchecked, with no system in place to process or vet them. Then, they later see a news article describing how existing policy requires stringent background checks for all refugees. Accepting the new information in the article could leave that person with an "incomplete event model" of an *effect* (refugees overwhelming the system) without a *cause* (unchecked entry) to explain it. Thus, people may be hesitant to accept corrections of policy misperceptions if doing so will undermine their mental model of how the policy works.

Resistance based in partisan identity

Over the past decade, the question of how to effectively correct political misperceptions has been a major focus of research (Berinsky 2017; Nyhan

2010; Schaffner and Luks 2018; Swire et al. 2017; Thorson 2016; Southwell et al. 2018). The good news is that overall, corrections work: people respond to factual information by becoming more accurate. However, this effectiveness comes with a caveat: people are less likely to accept a correction when it conflicts with a key part of their identity (Flynn et al. 2017; Kahan et al. 2017). When it comes to politics, the identity in question is most often partisanship. For example, in 2020, a viral post on Facebook inaccurately stated that then-vice-presidential candidate Kamala Harris was planning to sign an executive order to send people door-to-door collecting every gun in the United States (Czopek 2020). This piece of misinformation touches on two central aspects of Republican identity: dislike for a prominent Democratic candidate, and support for gun rights. Therefore, we might expect Republicans to be more resistant to corrections of the Harris executive order misinformation than Democrats.

Of course, political information (and misinformation) varies in how closely it is tied to partisanship. Much of the misinformation on fact-checking websites, including viral memes about hot-button political issues and statements by political figures, is deliberately designed to appeal to partisan identity. However, misperceptions about existing policy are not always so clear-cut in how (and whether) they reinforce partisan identities. For the most part, Republicans and Democrats are equally likely to hold the misperceptions identified in Chapter 2, but there are exceptions. Democrats are more likely than Republicans to underestimate the tax rate on the wealthy, and Republicans are more likely than Democrats to overestimate the size of the government. These patterns make intuitive sense: the idea that the rich pay too little in taxes is a key part of the Democratic platform, and the idea that the government is too large is similarly foundational for Republicans. Especially given this heterogeneity in the invented state, it is important to carefully assess the extent to which partisanship influences correction acceptance.

Why people may be indifferent to policy corrections

The previous section suggested that a policy correction might fail to increase accuracy if it attacks a belief that is so central to a person's mental model or partisan identity that they are reluctant to accept the new information. But policy corrections could also fail in another way: if people do not care enough about the topic to bother updating their beliefs. Below, I outline two reasons that information about existing policy may fail to capture the public's attention.

People don't care about policy

There is a long-standing belief among many journalists and pundits that people simply do not care about policy. As the *Washington Post* put it in a 2015 headline, "Voters Don't Really Care About Policy" (Cillizza 2015). To the extent that this belief has been empirically tested, it is largely by comparing public attention to policy focused versus strategy focused, or "game frame," coverage. Results are inconsistent: while some studies show that the public does indeed prefer strategy coverage (Iyengar et al. 2004), others show a preference for issue coverage (Jang and Oh 2016).

One explanation for these mixed results may be that public preference varies by context. In the height of a campaign, people might reasonably be focused on political strategy. But during other times, public attention might shift to issues. In addition, as discussed in Chapter 3, the category of "policy coverage" encompasses a huge variety of content, including information about candidates' issue stances and policy proposals, coverage of policy debates, and analyses of policy outcomes. People may well gravitate to some types of policy content over others. Preferences may also vary by issue, with people being more interested in substantive news coverage of policies that directly affect them.

Given these mixed results, and the dominance of the "Americans don't care about policy" narrative, it is especially important to test not only whether people believe policy corrections immediately after they receive them but also whether they process them deeply enough to recall them after time has passed.

Policy-current information is not novel

In addition to being potentially uninteresting, information about existing policy may face an additional barrier to public attention: it is usually old news. In Chapter 3, I suggest that journalists often fail to include policy-current information in their coverage because they prioritize novelty and conflict in their coverage. For example, during the 2012 presidential election, the media were more likely to report on polls that showed sudden shifts in which candidate was in the lead and less likely to report on those that showed a fairly stable race (Searles et al. 2016). Policy proposals like the Alexandria Ocasio-Cortez's 2019 "Green New Deal" or Donald Trump's 2016 call to "build the wall" are both novel and contentious. Policy outcomes, like the unemployment or uninsured rate, are both novel and dynamic. In contrast, details about existing policy, especially ones implemented years ago, are neither novel, contentious, nor dynamic. If journalists are correct that these news qualities are key to capturing public attention (Shoemaker 1996), then the public may simply ignore information about long-standing policy.

Assessing the effectiveness of policy-current corrections

This section attempts to answer the question of whether providing people with information about existing policy actually changes their factual beliefs. I present the results from two studies that first expose people to corrective information about existing policy, then assess whether this correction improved their accuracy. In many interventions designed to correct misperceptions, participants' beliefs are only measured immediately after the correction is administered. However, this practice may lead to overestimates of effect size because it ignores the potential for the effects to decay over time (Mutz 2011). To address this issue, both studies described in this section are panel surveys that followed the same basic format: respondents were asked a series of factual questions, then given the correct answers. About a month later, they were re-contacted and asked the same questions again. In other words, the dependent variable (belief) was measured nearly four weeks after the treatment (a correction) was administered.

The experiments were administered via the CCES (Comparative Congressional Election Survey), in 2014 (Study 1) and 2018 (Study 2). As described in more detail in Chapter 2, each of the factual questions in the surveys were asked in a format designed to minimize acquiescence bias as well as measure confidence. Respondents were told, "You will be presented with eight pairs of statements. In each pair, one statement is true and one statement is false. Please select the statement that you think is most correct." After choosing the statement they thought was more correct, a pop-up question asked them how confident they were in their answer. Table 7.1 shows the misperceptions measured in each study.[1]

After answering the factual questions, participants were told, "Next, you will see the correct answers to the questions you answered earlier." Then, they were shown the correct answer for each question, each on a separate page. In the second wave of the survey, administered about a month after the first wave, all respondents answered the same series of factual questions in the same format.

In the 2014 survey, one-third of the sample was randomly assigned *not* to receive the answers in the first wave of the survey. Because this group was asked the questions again in the second wave of the survey, they serve as a control group, to help ensure that any increase in correct answers in the second wave was due to the corrections in the first wave rather than learning from the external environment.

Table 7.1 shows the misperceptions measured in each study, as well as their prevalence (as measured in Wave 1). Four were measured in both studies, five only in Study 1, and four only in Study 2.[2] The table shows the

Table 7.1 Misperception prevalence in Study 1 (2014) and Study 2 (2018)

Misperception	2014	2018
China holds more than half of U.S. debt.	68%	68%
Interest on the federal debt is more than half of federal spending.	63%	66%
Currently, there is no federal limit on how long a person can receive welfare (TANF) benefits.	52%	54%
Less than 25% of food stamp recipients are children.	30%	N/A
The government spends more on the military than on healthcare.	63%	N/A
Compared to ten years ago, the percentage of Americans employed by the federal government has increased.	51%	N/A
Undocumented immigrants are eligible to receive food stamps.	56%	52%
Social Security benefits are paid for by money that retired people contributed to their Social Security savings account while they were employed.	40%	N/A
A person who makes over $500,000 a year pays less than 25% of their income in taxes.	46%	N/A
Federal law requires licensed gun dealers to conduct background checks.	N/A	23%
In the U.S., corporations are taxed at a lower rate than in most other developed countries.	N/A	43%
Planned Parenthood receives federal funding and is allowed to use it to provide abortion services.	N/A	51%

total percentage of people giving the incorrect answer, regardless of their initial level of confidence.

Table 7.1 also shows that among the four misperceptions measured in both studies, there is remarkable consistency. Despite the passage of four years between the studies, fewer than 4 percentage points separate the percentage of people who hold the misperception. This stability is consistent with the idea that these misperceptions may not be a product of the external information environment.

Can policy misperceptions be corrected?

The corrective intervention in this experiment consisted of a single statement briefly shown after the respondent had answered each factual question. A month later, participants were re-contacted and asked the factual question again. Panel surveys testing the over-time effects of corrective interventions have yielded mixed results. Some studies show that effects of corrections on accuracy disappear over time (Carey et al. 2022), while others show more enduring effects (Carnahan et al. 2021).

Figure 7.1 shows the change in the proportion of participants holding the misperception between Wave 1 and Wave 2 (Table 7.2 shows the percentage answering incorrectly in each wave). Negative numbers correspond to a decrease in misperceptions. In every area but one (that corporations in the U.S. are taxed at a lower rate than corporations in other developed countries), the corrections significantly reduced misperceptions. For example, in Wave 1 of Study 2, 52% of respondents stated that there was no federal limit on how long a person could receive TANF benefits. In Wave 2, just 28% of respondents answered incorrectly. Exposing people to corrections of policy misperceptions substantially increases accuracy, even a month after the corrective intervention.

However, because these data are observational, it is possible that the differences between Wave 1 and Wave 2 are attributable to external changes in the information environment that occurred in the month between the two waves. This alternative explanation can be addressed by leveraging the "control group" that was a part of Study 1's design. In Study 1, one-third of the sample did not receive the correct answers in Wave 1. Among this group, for each misperception, the percentage who answered incorrectly in Wave 2 is statistically indistinguishable from the percentage of people in the treatment

124 THE INVENTED STATE

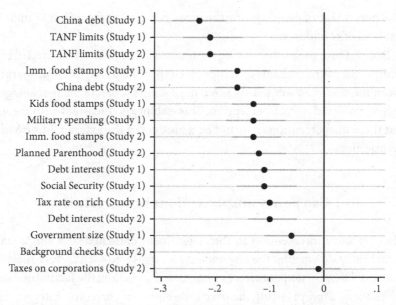

Figure 7.1 Change in proportion of people holding misperceptions (Wave 1–Wave 2)

condition who answered incorrectly at Wave 1. In other words, there is no evidence of learning between waves. While there was not a similar control group in Study 2, the consistency of these results suggests that the information environment does not actively correct misperceptions about existing policy.

Figure 7.1 includes people who were very confident, somewhat confident, and not at all confident in their incorrect answers. Thus, the observed effect could be attributable to learning (whereby people who guessed incorrectly subsequently learned the correct answer), a correction effect (whereby people who were initially confident in their wrong answer accepted the correction and changed their belief accordingly), or a combination of both. In addition, because Figure 7.1 shows just the difference in means between Wave 1 and Wave 2, it does not take into account how partisanship might have shaped how people responded to the corrective information.

To examine how both confidence and partisan identity affect a person's willingness to accept and recall the correction, for each question I predict a correct answer in Wave 2 among those who were incorrect in Wave 1. The models also include education and ideology (on a 1–5 scale) from "very liberal" to "very conservative."[3] Modeling each answer separately (as opposed to combining them into a larger index of misperceptions) recognizes that not all questions are equally tied to partisan identity, and those that are vary in the direction of that bias.

In Table 7.2, the first two columns show the percentage of people holding the misperception in the first and the second waves. The final three columns show whether answering correctly in Wave 2 (among those who were incorrect in Wave 1) was significantly associated with confidence, education, or ideology ($p < .05$).

For five out of the 16 misperceptions, there is a significant negative association with confidence: those who were more confident in Wave 1 were less likely to answer correctly in Wave 2. For about a third of the issues, the increase in accuracy was concentrated among those who were less confident in Wave 1, but in the majority, confidence in Wave 1 was not significantly associated with a correct answer in Wave 2. This pattern suggests that the observed effect of the intervention is likely due to a combination of both

Table 7.2 The effects of confidence, education, and ideology on correctability

	Wave 1	Wave 2	Confidence	Education	Ideology
China debt (Study 1)	68%	45%	√–	√+	
China debt (Study 2)	68%	46%	√–	√+	
Military spending	63%	50%		√+	
Debt interest (Study 1)	63%	52%	√–	√+	
Debt interest (Study 2)	63%	52%		√+	
Imm. food stamps (Study 1)	56%	40%			
Imm. food stamps (Study 2)	56%	37%		√+	
TANF limits (Study 1)	52%	31%			
TANF limits (Study 2)	54%	29%			
Planned Parenthood funding	51%	37%			
Government size	51%	45%	√–		
Tax rate on wealthy	46%	36%		√+	
Taxes on corporations	43%	42%			√–
Social Security	40%	30%			
Kids food stamps	30%	17%			
Background checks	23%	17%	√–	√+	

correction and learning. When it comes to policy misperceptions, many people who are initially quite confident in their incorrect answer are willing to accept corrective information.

The overall pattern is even more clear when it comes to ideology: in only one case (the corporate tax rate) is ideology significantly associated with correction acceptance. Given the intense concern over how motivated reasoning shapes factual beliefs and responses to corrective interventions, it is worth emphasizing that ideology plays a largely nonexistent role in the effectiveness of the policy corrections tested here. However, in some ways this pattern should not be surprising in light of this book's findings. As outlined in Chapter 3, the media often fail to accurately cover the facts of existing policy partly because these pieces of information do not easily fit into their focus on political competition and novelty. By the same token, politicians have little interest in rehashing the details of existing policy: it is in their strategic interest to talk about the effects of policies (the abortion rate, the crime rate) or their proposals for change, rather than to offer details of how current policies actually work. While the disinterest of both the media and politicians in discussing existing policy provides fertile ground for misperceptions to flourish, it also means that these misperceptions are less likely to be explicitly or implicitly tied to partisan identity.

Finally, for half of the misperceptions, there is a significant positive association with education: among those who answered incorrectly in Wave 1, those with more education are more likely to answer correctly in Wave 2. In some ways, this association makes intuitive sense: we might expect people with more existing knowledge to both pay more attention to information about policy and be able to integrate it into their existing knowledge structure. However, it is worth noting that this pattern runs counter to other work showing that education (and political sophistication more generally) is associated with *more* resistance to corrective information, particularly around highly politicized issues like climate change and gun control (Kahan 2015). Education can increase resistance to politically charged issues in two ways: by helping people recognize "what goes with what," so that they can quickly grasp whether a particular correction reinforces or contradicts their partisan commitments, and by helping them generate counterarguments that allow them to resist the correction (Flynn et al. 2016). The fact that when it comes to policy misperceptions, the more educated are consistently *more* correctable provides additional evidence for the hypothesis (also explored in Chapter 5) that misperceptions about existing policy are less likely to encourage partisan interpretation.

Is there public demand for policy-current information?

Studies 1 and 2 show that, when exposed to corrective information about existing policy, people pay attention and recall it, even a month later. However, one weakness of these studies is that they are "forced-exposure" experiments in which participants are obligated to read and process the information (Arceneaux and Johnson 2013). A reasonable concern is that if journalists were to publish news articles about existing policy and/or integrate it into existing coverage, people would simply ignore the information. Therefore, this section presents two studies that assess different dimensions of public attention to policy-current information. The first tests public interest by asking participants to choose between reading a policy-current, policy-potential, or policy-outcome news story. The second tests the effectiveness of embedding policy-current information in traditional news coverage.

Study 1: Measuring public appetite for policy-current coverage

A total of 966 respondents were recruited by Lucid.[4] After answering several demographic questions, respondents were randomly assigned to one of four policy topics (Medicare policy, education policy, refugee policy, or environmental policy). They were then told, "As part of this survey, you may be asked to carefully read one of three brief news article about [policy]. Below are the headlines of the three articles. We'd like you to know which one you'd prefer to read. Please rank the three articles below." Rather than simply asking "what type of news do you prefer?" (which might induce social desirability bias), the question was designed to suggest that participants were making a choice with in-survey consequences.

The headlines took the same format regardless of the issue area. They were presented in random order and designed to speak to the three types of policy coverage identified in Chapter 3: policy-current, policy-potential, and policy-outcome.

128 THE INVENTED STATE

- Three Key Facts About Current [Policy]
- Three Key Facts About the Republican and Democratic [Policy] Proposals
- Three Key Facts About the Effects of [Policy]

To create a measure of average preference for each article, I assign a score of 3 if it is ranked first, and 1 if it is ranked last. Figure 7.2 shows the average preference score for each article, combining across all issues. Respondents showed a significantly stronger preference for the article describing existing policy ("Three Key Facts About Current [Policy]"). This pattern holds within each topic area: for each of the four topics, the policy-current article is the most popular. The policy-potential article ("Three Key Facts About the Republican and Democratic [Policy] Proposals") takes second place for three out of the four topics, followed by the policy-outcome article.

These results suggest that despite what journalists might believe, there is a strong public appetite for news coverage of existing policy, and that demand for this type of news can even outstrip demand for coverage focusing on policy proposals or policy outcomes.

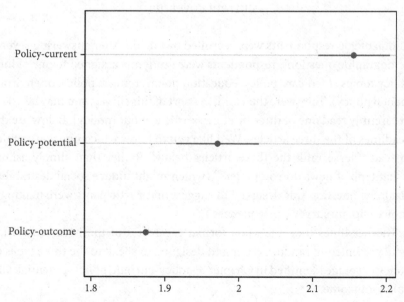

Figure 7.2 Average preference for policy article types

Table 7.3 examines factors associated with a preference for the policy-current, policy-potential, and policy-outcome articles. Specifically, it includes a range of characteristics that tend to be associated with news preferences, including party identification (reference category: independents), political interest, political knowledge, education, and gender.

Compared to Independents, partisans express more interest in reading the article describing Republican and Democratic policy proposals. Political interest is also negatively associated with interest in the policy-current article and positively with the policy-potential article.

Overall, Table 7.3 suggests that the highly politically involved are especially interested in the partisan competition aspect of, whereas the less politically involved prefer coverage of existing policy. This pattern could pose a challenge for news organizations looking to expand their policy-current coverage since news audiences tend to be politically engaged. Still, it is worth noting that policy-current coverage is popular even among this group: those who say they follow politics "very" or "somewhat" closely still express a slight (though nonsignificant) preference for policy-current coverage ($M = 2.1$, SE $=.03$) over policy-potential coverage ($M = 2.0$, SE $= .03$). While coverage of existing policy appeals to all segments of the public, coverage of policy proposals appeals most strongly to those who are already heavily invested in partisan politics.

Table 7.3 Factors associated with policy news preference

	Policy-current		Policy-potential		Policy-outcome	
Republican	−0.22**	(0.077)	0.47***	(0.086)	−0.25***	(0.073)
Democrat	−0.12	(0.075)	0.27**	(0.085)	−0.15*	(0.071)
Political interest	−0.069*	(0.033)	0.079*	(0.037)	−0.0098	(0.031)
Political knowledge	−0.0024	(0.029)	0.019	(0.032)	−0.017	(0.027)
Education	−0.020	(0.032)	0.059	(0.036)	−0.039	(0.030)
Female	0.076	(0.052)	−0.0066	(0.059)	−0.069	(0.050)
Constant	2.53***	(0.14)	1.24***	(0.15)	2.24***	(0.13)
Observations	966		966		966	
Adjusted R^2	0.016		0.041		0.011	

Note: Standard errors in parentheses
*$p < .05$, **$p < .01$, ***$p < .001$

Study 2: Contextual fact-checking in practice

So far in this chapter, I have suggested that offering corrective policy information in the context of an article can be effective at reducing misperceptions and will not alienate news consumers. This section presents the results of another test of this argument. I randomly assign 275 participants, recruited via Mechanical Turk, to see one of two different versions of a news article (ostensibly from *USA Today*) about the national debt. The versions are nearly identical, with one exception: the treatment article included a box with information correcting common misperceptions about the national debt. The articles were designed to be as realistic as possible, including reproducing the typeface and format used by the newspaper. The treatment article is shown in Figure 7.3. The text of the control article was identical, but without the "What is the national debt?" box.

After reading the article, participants were first asked about how (very much, somewhat, not at all) they felt when reading the article along five dimensions: frustrated, confused, informed, calm, and satisfied. The five items formed a reliable scale ($\alpha = .69$, $M = 2.1$, SE $= .02$). They were then asked two factual questions: whether interest on the national debt was more or less than half the U.S. budget, and whether China owned more or less than half the national debt.

Participants who saw the article containing the contextual fact-check were significantly more likely to answer the questions correctly than those

Trump Budget Proposal Receives Mixed Response

Cuts to domestic programs with the goal of debt reduction.

Jacob O'Malley
USA TODAY

The Trump administration released a budget proposal on Tuesday that includes substantial cuts to domestic programs and an increase in military spending. The administration says that the proposed budget would allow the government to pay back the entire $20 trillion national debt over the next thirty years.

However, the non-partisan Committee for a Responsible Federal Budget questioned the administration's calculations. They estimate that Trump's plan to cut corporate and individual taxes would actually cost the federal government about $5.5 trillion over 10 years, adding more than $6 trillion to the national debt.

The budget met with mixed responses from members of Congress. House Speaker Paul Ryan (R-WI) said the budget was "right on target," while Senator John McCain (R-AZ) declared it "dead on arrival." House Minority Leader Nancy Pelosi (D-CA) charged that the budget is based on "bogus" economic projections.

What is the national debt?
The U.S. national debt is the total debt owed by the federal government. The government owes **most** of its debt to U.S. citizens, state governments, and the Federal Reserve. A **third** of the debt is owed to other nations. Interest on the debt is about **six percent** of the U.S. budget.

Figure 7.3 Treatment article containing contextual fact-check

who read the same article without the fact-check. The average score in the treatment group was 1.2 (out of 2) compared to .7 in the control group. In addition, they reported more positive emotions (along each of the five dimensions) when reading the article, although the overall difference was only marginally significant ($p = .062$).

The results of this brief experiment suggest that adding just a few additional sentences to policy coverage can substantially improve readers' understanding of complex issues, as well as potentially increase their positive feelings toward the news—an especially important effect in a time when many readers feel overwhelmed by the information environment (Toff and Kalogeropoulos 2020).

Conclusion

In the introduction to this chapter, I outlined two reasons why corrective interventions aimed at reducing policy misperceptions might not work. The first is resistance: people might be unwilling to accept information that contradicts their existing beliefs, especially if those beliefs are closely tied to their partisan identity. However, the results from two panel studies suggest that partisanship is largely irrelevant in how people process corrections of policy-current information. Because the misperceptions that make up the invented state are often (though not always) less politicized than those that are the focus of most media and academic attention, corrections work across party lines.

The second potential barrier to successfully correcting policy misperceptions is indifference. If, as many pundits assume, people do not care about policy, then they may not bother to process or recall policy-relevant corrections. The first study in this chapter is a difficult test of the "stickiness" of policy-current corrections. Unlike in most survey experiments, a full month passed between the corrective interventions and the follow-up questions measuring knowledge. Despite this gap in time, the corrections were consistently effective in increasing accuracy.

Finally, a survey asking people to choose between reading a news article featuring policy-current, policy-outcome, or policy-potential coverage suggests that there is a real public appetite for information about existing policy. Across four very different issue areas (Medicare, education, refugees, and the environment) people express a strong preference for news coverage focused on *current* policy (rather than proposed policy or policy outcomes). Taken together, the results of these studies suggest that contrary to pundits' assumptions of a public who is largely indifferent to politics, there is a deep public desire to learn basic facts about how policy works.

8
Conclusion
What comes next?

On the surface, this book may appear to be part of a long (and often rather patronizing) tradition of pointing out how very much the public gets wrong about politics. In Chapter 2, I detail a number of widespread misperceptions about existing public policy, and a reader might be reasonably concerned that I am joining the ranks of the public-shaming. But I depart from this narrative in Chapter 3, arguing that people often get the facts wrong about existing policy not because they are lazy, stupid, or blinded by partisan loyalty. Rather, this information is largely unavailable to them. News coverage—even when specifically about policy issues—does not regularly include information about *existing* policy. Instead, policy coverage prioritizes strategy, novelty, and change. While this focus is understandable, it also creates critical gaps in the information environment. Casual consumers of the news will likely not encounter many details about current policies, even those that impact their lives in meaningful ways.

I argue in Chapter 4 that when faced with these gaps in their knowledge, many people make a valiant effort to fill them in on their own. They engage in inductive reasoning about policy, using both cues from the environment (sometimes including misleading information from elites) and their own cognitive heuristics to generate inferences about what the government actually does. Unfortunately, many of these inferences are incorrect.

While the first half of the book traces the origins of the invented state, the second explores how these policy misperceptions shape attitudes and whether they can be effectively corrected. In Chapter 5, I show that when people see corrective information about existing policy, they are less likely to interpret it through a partisan lens than when they see corrective information about policy *outcomes*. This lack of partisan-driven motivated reasoning increases the likelihood of policy-current information having downstream effects on attitudes. Chapter 6 investigates that process in more detail and finds that providing people basic descriptive information about an existing policy not only increases their approval but also changes how they prioritize different aspects of the policy.

Chapter 7 explores two potential roadblocks to dismantling the invented state: resistance and indifference. To what extent does partisan identity and/or a lack of interest in policy limit the effects of corrective interventions? A popular narrative suggests that Americans simply don't care about policy, and so attempts to correct policy misperceptions will inevitably go in one ear and out the other. However, I show that when people are provided with corrective information about existing policy, they remain more accurate even a month later. In addition, people express a strong preference for news coverage of existing policy over news coverage of policy proposals or policy outcomes.

I begin this final chapter by explaining some of the contributions I hope this book makes to the larger conversation about knowledge, misinformation, and citizen competence. I also consider some of the book's limitations, including questions it leaves unanswered. Finally, I offer some practical suggestions for how both journalists and academics might build on these findings to begin to dismantle the invented state.

Policy misperceptions and competence

The data collection for this book spans almost eight years, making it a relatively brief snapshot of public beliefs and attitudes. The specific policy misperceptions I identify and analyze in this book may well disappear in a decade, or even sooner. The primary contribution of this book is not the particular set of policy misperceptions it identifies but rather the principles they illustrate: that policy misperceptions can arise from internal as well as external sources, that they pose a threat to democratic functioning, and that we should pay more attention to understanding and correcting them.

For the past decade, many intellectual and financial resources have been directed at stanching the flow of highly politicized misinformation entering the information ecosystem. While this research is important, the misperceptions created by "fake news" are not the only misperceptions that matter. From the point of view of improving democratic competence, policy misperceptions are potentially massive in both magnitude and effects. And from a practical perspective, policy misperceptions are low-hanging fruit. Unlike many highly politicized misperceptions (e.g., Barack Obama's birthplace), they are eminently correctable—and more importantly, those corrections have downstream effects on attitudes. Below I summarize three major contributions this book makes to the ongoing conversation about what people know, don't know, and get wrong about politics.

A new methodological approach for identifying widespread misperceptions

In my course on experimental design, students often struggle to identify testable hypothesis. To help, I ask them to compile a list of interesting or novel things in the world (e.g., dance videos on TikTok, electric cars, or mask mandates) and then imagine what the effects of those things might be. How does the world look different because these things exist? Completing this exercise helps them generate a host of intriguing hypotheses. This approach is intuitive and often illuminating, and it is especially helpful for identifying causal questions about media effects.

A great deal of research on misperceptions (including much of my own work) takes a similar approach. First, researchers identify novel pieces of misinformation "in the wild," including "fake news" websites, social media posts, and elite fabrications. Then, they design surveys and experiments to measure the extent to which people believe the misinformation and/or whether it can be corrected. Much of what we know about misperceptions comes from these types of studies, which often ask about highly circulated and/or newsworthy pieces of misinformation. For example, between 2008 and 2015, at least 36 different public opinion polls asked respondents whether Barack Obama was a Muslim.[1]

This book takes a different approach. First, I draw a clear line between misinformation (false information) and misperceptions (false beliefs). Then, instead of starting by identifying pieces of misinformation in the world, I instead seek to identify misperceptions that exist inside peoples' heads, using interviews in which I asked people to talk to me about their factual beliefs. In later chapters, I use open-ended responses in a similar way. Of course, this participant-led approach to identifying modes of thinking is not novel—for example, Cramer (2016) uses it to identify an urban-rural cleavage in political opinion. By demonstrating how a bottom-up approach can be used to identify not only *opinions* but also *factual beliefs*, this book adds to the methodological toolbox researchers use to construct models of public knowledge.

The strategy of seeking to identify false *beliefs* rather than just false *information* can also be employed using methods other than interviews. For example, systematically tracking social media mentions of policies (e.g., with keywords like "WIC" or "Social Security") could identify common misperceptions, and analyses of comments on news stories or posts could also reveal areas of confusion. And while open-ended questions on surveys are often used as a space for people to expand their opinions, they can also be used as a prompt for articulating factual beliefs.

A focus on opinions, not just beliefs

In addition to its methodological contribution, this book also attempts to change the conversation about misperceptions to include a deliberate focus on downstream attitudinal effects. In 1995, Michael Delli Carpini and Scott Keeter published *What Americans Know About Politics and Why It Matters*. This book is a classic because in addition to systematically identifying what people know about politics, it also attempts to connect that knowledge to opinion and behavior. But often, this two-step process has not been applied to the study of misinformation. Many scholars and pundits are deeply concerned about misinformation, but too infrequently ask the difficult question of when and whether it has a causal impact on attitudes and/or behavior (McGregor and Kreiss 2020).

The simplest approach to measuring this causal impact would be to give people misinformation and then measure its downstream effects on opinion. However, this approach is problematic for two reasons. First, there are ethical concerns with deliberately exposing people to misinformation, especially given its potential lasting effects on beliefs and attitudes (Thorson 2016). Second, as detailed in Chapter 4, many of the policy misperceptions this book explores are not the product of external misinformation but rather of internal cognitive processes. Thus, exposing people to a statement like "TANF benefits are time-unlimited" does not replicate the real-world experience of how these misperceptions are formed.

Therefore, the second half of the book presents a range of experiments that assign participants to receive *corrections* of common policy misperceptions, and then examine the effects of these corrections on downstream opinions. "But wait!" an astute reader might say. "This experimental design means that you cannot say for certain whether your treatment is correcting misperceptions or remedying ignorance." This astute reader is absolutely correct. And indeed, I suspect that both processes are occurring. Belief is a spectrum, and the line between "ignorance" and "misperception" is often quite blurry. However, when large numbers of people answer a policy question incorrectly, this pattern sends a meaningful signal about the state of public knowledge even if not every person who answered incorrectly holds a strong, stable false belief. Some people who answered incorrectly might fervently believe the misperceptions. Some might hold the belief more tentatively. Others may never have thought about the issue before reading the question but made an incorrect inference when asked to provide an answer. This book is largely agnostic about which one of those people "really" hold misperceptions, partly because this distinction becomes less important when our normative concern is downstream effects on *opinion*. Our standard for whether a misperception is problematic should be whether and how it distorts attitudes. This approach follows directly from a long line of reasoning about political ignorance: ignorance is only a problem insofar as it prevents people from making political decisions that are in line with their values (Lupia 2015; Althaus 2006).

To sum up, when we see that X% of the population answers a factual survey question incorrectly, we should not interpret this number as meaning that X% of the population confidently holds a false belief; rather, it is signaling a mix of false belief, confusion, and incorrect inference. It is also a signal that competence may be threatened, and the next step should be to test for a causal link between this incorrect answer and related opinions.

Currently, the academic focus on misperceptions has been almost exclusively on how "fake news," fact-checks, and other novel phenomena affect false beliefs among the American public. While these efforts are undeniably important, this line of research should be expanded to encompass not only the effects of misinformation but also the creation and impact of *misperceptions*—including those that do not come from explicit misinformation.

A more optimistic assessment of the public's appetite for policy

It is a truism in the pundit class that people do not care about public policy, but it is a truism with surprisingly little empirical support. And indeed, the results presented in this book suggest a very different reality. People care about policy enough to spend cognitive energy making (sometimes incorrect) inferences about it. They care about policy enough to remember corrective information about it in a survey, even a month later. They care about policy enough to express a consistent preference for news coverage about it. Each of these findings on its own is not conclusive, but taken together they paint a picture of a citizenry who actually *does* care about public policy and, in particular, about the details of existing policy. The public has a real interest in better understanding what the government actually does. Policy corrections work, and work well. These findings are a promising start to designing interventions that increase competence.

What more do we need to know?

First, while the surveys and experiments in this book cover a wide range of issue areas, they are by no means exhaustive, and the book largely ignores huge swaths of public policy. To name a few important omissions: education, tax credits, public infrastructure, and energy. All of these policy areas directly impact most Americans, and misperceptions about them may be common. While it is beyond the scope of this book to identify every widely held policy misperception, my hope is that it outlines a clear process for future scholars to (1) identify misperceptions, (2) test the extent to which correcting them has downstream effects on opinions, and (3) design effective corrections.

This book also does little to explore systematic variation between different policy areas and, in particular, the extent to which a policy is intertwined with partisanship. In Chapter 2, I suggest that the politicization of a particular misperception (in other words, how much it reinforces partisan identity) might affect both who believes it and its correctability, as well as offer some initial observational evidence that this is the case.

Understanding how partisan politics affect policy misperceptions matters in part because politicians can help create policy misperceptions even without explicitly spreading misinformation. For example, a politician might attempt to make their policy proposals appear more important by denigrating existing policies, even at the cost of stretching the truth. During his 2016 presidential campaign, Donald Trump gave a speech arguing that "the time has come for a new immigration commission to develop a new set of reforms to our legal immigration system in order to achieve the following goals," among which he included "keeping immigration levels within historical norms" and allowing immigrants to enter the U.S. based on their "likelihood of success" (Timms 2016). Neither of these statements contain explicit misinformation, but they strongly imply that *existing* U.S. immigration levels were far off from historical levels (they were not) and that the admission process did not take into consideration applicants' education or skills (it does). Because, as Chapter 3 describes, the media tend to devote more attention to politicians' proposals than to existing policy, there is plenty of room for Trump's misleading rhetoric to help create misperceptions.

What should we do?

Throughout the book, I suggest that informational interventions can help eliminate misperceptions and increase democratic competence. But how might designing and implementing these interventions work in the real world? The following section discusses how dismantling the invented state can fit within existing journalistic practices.

Integrating policy-current information into media coverage

Chapter 3 argues that the media often fail to provide information about existing policy. Including more coverage of existing policy upends the traditional models of political coverage (which tends to focus on strategy and game frames, to the exclusion of policy content) and policy coverage (which tends to focus on novelty and change to the exclusion of current policy). Policy-current coverage does not fit neatly into an existing category of news, as it is almost never "breaking," except in the brief moments after a new policy is enacted. However, the idea of providing news consumers with basic contextual information is closely related to several other journalistic formats: explanatory journalism and service journalism.

Media institutions have long recognized the need for clear, accessible explanations of complex topics. In 1984, the Pulitzer Prize Board announced the creation of a new prize: "Explanatory Reporting." The prize was created partly because the Board saw a need for journalism that clarified and explained an increasingly complicated political world (Forde 2007). Thirty years later, Melissa Bell, Ezra Klein, and Matt Yglesias founded Vox.com with the explicit goal of helping people "understand the news better" (Carr 2014). This genre, which they dubbed "explainer journalism," expands the Pulitzer committee's directive to an online format with the goal of providing readers with the context and background they need to understand complicated issues. Vox.com has since been joined by other "explainer" websites, including the Upshot column in the *New York Times* (Moses 2014).

Since explanatory journalism is written to provide *context* to the news (which often involves policy proposals and outcomes), information about existing policy is a natural fit. To understand a candidate's plan to reform refugee admissions, we need to know what the current admission process looks like. To understand why the percentage of people with health insurance is increasing, we need to know about the Affordable Care Act's insurance mandate.

Information about existing policy can also fit into the category of "service journalism," in which media outlets provide their audiences with information to help them with problems in their everyday life (Eide and Knight 1999; Usher 2012). Because many current policies directly affect peoples' lives, some news stories that include policy-current information can also be seen as a form of service journalism. For example, a feature explaining how to navigate the tax system is service journalism as well as providing a clear explanation of existing policy.

However, making a commitment to including more coverage of existing policy can be even simpler than engaging in full-blown explanatory or service journalism. Information about existing policy can easily be integrated into existing coverage. One approach might be to first identify common misperceptions about a particular policy and to use those to create a set of "background facts" that are then included in coverage of that policy. For example, Chapter 2 identifies several misperceptions about the TANF program that could easily be corrected with a few sentences added to any article that mentions the program.

Making a concerted effort to include descriptive information about existing policy could also attract new audiences. Chapter 7 shows that when given the choice people actively prefer articles focusing on existing policy to those focusing on policy outcomes or policy proposals, and this preference holds across a range of issues. Including more information about existing policy could attract new readers, especially those who are turned off by an intense focus on partisanship (Klar and Krupnikov 2016).

Of course, media outlets need to balance the opportunity to attract new readers with the need to satisfy existing ones, and evidence suggests that the highly politically involved often prefer strategy coverage to policy coverage (Trussler and Soroka 2014). However, including corrective information about existing policy is not incompatible with strategy coverage. For example, a piece focused on how a candidate's immigration proposal is hurting her in the polls could also include a brief description of existing immigration policy. Many existing studies of news coverage frame strategy versus policy as an "either/or" choice, but, especially in the age of online news, space is no longer as constrained, and the two types of coverage can be more easily combined. As "explainer journalist" David Roberts puts it, "There are no longer supply constraints—it is trivially cheap and easy to publish something on the web—and there are virtually no constraints left on the supply of information" (Roberts 2019).

In addition, social media provides an alternative way of issuing "corrections" to commonly held policy misperceptions. News outlets' social media accounts could, along with posting links to breaking news, create social media content that provides the background information necessary for understanding that news. Adding this content might also help reduce the perceived "information overload" that diminishes many peoples' ability to effectively learn from news on social media (Van Erkel and Van Aelst 2021).

For example, in June of 2022, the North Carolina State Senate passed a bill that would expand Medicaid coverage, and the bill then went to the House. The Twitter account of the state's largest newspaper, the *News and Observer* (based out of Raleigh, NC) posted several links to the outlet's coverage of the ongoing debate. Figure 8.1 shows a tweet from June 29 describing a state legislator's decision to support Medicaid expansion.

While this tweet is effective at keeping dedicated readers up to date on breaking news, it is likely largely incomprehensible to people who have been following the issue closely. Contextualizing this post with additional tweets explaining exactly what Medicaid is and what "expansion" means could have dispelled misperceptions as well as made the article itself more accessible.

Unfortunately, identifying common misperceptions about policy may be easier said than done. Media outlets are engaged in an ongoing struggle to determine what, exactly, their readers want (Ferrer-Conill and Tandoc 2018). While newsrooms increasingly rely on quantitative sources like clicks and shares (Carlson 2018), they also generalize from their own experience and that of people they know (Usher 2021). The tendency for journalists to

Figure 8.1 Tweet from the *North Carolina News and Observer*

rely on their own experiences in curating and explaining the news is one of the reasons that so many have agitated to improve diversity in newsrooms on a range of dimensions, including race, gender, and location (e.g., urban vs. rural) (Burns 2022). There has not, however, been a similar push for diversity in *political interest*. For obvious reasons, newsrooms tend not to hire people who do not know much about politics.

Given these challenges, the next section describes the practical steps involved in identifying commonly held misperceptions and then designing interventions to correct them.

Practical steps to identifying misperceptions

A news organization seeking to correct misperceptions about a given policy can begin by collecting information about the public's factual beliefs. If a data collection pipeline is already in place (e.g., regular reader surveys), this could be done by adding open-ended questions. Alternatively, they could conduct an ad hoc survey by including a link in a Facebook post or email to their readers. Interviews could also be helpful, though may be more time-intensive than other methods. Importantly, at this point data collection does not need to be perfectly representative (either of the outlet's audience or of the general population), since the goal is only to generate an *initial* list of areas of confusion or misperception. Regardless of the approach, the questions asked should probe respondents' *factual understanding* rather than their opinions: for example, "To the best of your knowledge, what did the American Rescue Plan do?"

Attention to elite rhetoric can also provide clues about potential misperceptions. Even if elites are not actively spreading misinformation, they may use misleading language that can help foster misperceptions. For example, immediately after the American Rescue Plan was passed, Rep. Liz Cheney (R-WY) suggested that it would be funded largely through middle-class tax increases (Robertson 2021). Her claim is not precisely false—the policy, like most, was largely unfunded, and so paying for it via middle-class tax increases was certainly an eventual possibility. However, a reasonable person might interpret her words (which were echoed by other Republicans) to mean that these tax increases were inevitable rather than possible, thus creating a misperception.

The next step is to assess the prevalence of the misperceptions generated via the open-ended approach with a representative survey. If, for example, multiple participants in the first stage of the project mentioned a belief that the American Rescue Plan made it illegal for landlords to evict tenants who don't pay rent, then that question should be included on the survey. The population of interest will vary depending on the news organization. An outlet may want to survey only its audience or cast a wider net by partnering with a survey firm.

Once a set of (relatively) common misperceptions about a particular policy has been identified, news organizations can design corrective interventions. The nature of this intervention will, of course, vary depending on the news outlet: a local TV news station will have different resources and affordances than an online newspaper. For a newspaper, a brief description of the policy that provides context and dispels misperceptions could be included as a call-out box included in any online article about the policy. If at all possible, this background information should be included directly in the story rather than being "opt-in." In other words, it should not only be accessible by clicking on the name of the policy or a "learn more" link at the end of the article. The idea is to provide people with the information they need *within the context of the story* rather than forcing them to go elsewhere.

Political satire and comedy like *Last Week Tonight With John Oliver* can provide an alternative model for how to integrate information about existing policy in a way that is both effective and compelling. Both observational and experimental studies suggest that viewing late-night comedy is associated with greater knowledge, including about issues that, like many of the policies that make up the invented state, are both mundane and fairly technical (e.g., campaign finance reform and net neutrality) (Becker and Bode 2018; Hardy et al. 2014).

Satire is an effective channel for political learning for several reasons, many of which are directly applicable to dismantling the invented state. First, writers and producers of these shows recognize that in order for their audience to "get" the joke, they must first provide the necessary context (Xenos and Becker 2009). This type of "scaffolding" is similar to the stated goal of explanatory journalism. Both push journalists to ask themselves what the audience needs to understand to fully and accurately grasp the issue at hand.

Conclusion

Despite explaining, in great detail, how much Americans get wrong about what the government actually does, this is a fundamentally optimistic book. Yes, people hold meaningful misperceptions about public policy—but they do so because they care enough about those policies to think and reason about them. And while these misperceptions do distort attitudes, they can be effectively corrected with relatively simple interventions. My hope is that this book not only sheds a new light on how Americans think about policy, but that it also serves as a blueprint for academics, journalists, and others who want to design evidence-based interventions to improve democratic competence.

Notes

Chapter 1

1. This is not to say that preferences are themselves exogenous to the external political world—of course, what information people access and how they interpret that information is enormously shaped by both internal factors (like partisanship) and external factors (like the media environment) (Druckman 2014).
2. Of course, this is not to say that conspiracy theories and misinformation are harmless: they may have other effects on democratic functioning, including increasing distrust in the political system and affective polarization (Lazer et al. 2018).

Chapter 2

1. In 2014, the year these interviews were conducted, the ten issues that topped the Gallup list were "Government/Congress/Politicians, Economy in general, Unemployment/jobs, Healthcare, Immigration, Federal deficit/debt, Ethics/Moral decline, Education, Poverty, and Focus Overseas." While social welfare programs are not specifically on this list, they are the policy responses to issues like poverty and healthcare (Saad 2015).
2. Names of interview subjects have been changed.
3. The survey also contained an embedded experiment in which a subsample of participants received corrections of the misinformation. This experiment is discussed in detail in Chapter 6.
4. Chapter 6 includes more detail on the respondents who answered the questions in the second wave, including analyses showing that they are not any more or less likely to answer the questions correctly than those who saw them in the first survey wave. In other words, there is no evidence for "learning" during the month between survey waves.
5. As Graham (2023) shows, even misperceptions held with a great deal of confidence may still be "mistaken inferences." Indeed, Chapter 4 demonstrates evidence of exactly this process.
6. $N = 5{,}375$ for the ANES analyses. Respondents were classified as holding the misperceptions if they said that the false statement was "definitely" or "probably" true. See Miller, Saunders, and Farhart (2016) for more detailed analyses of the distribution and correlates of these misperceptions.

Chapter 3

1. Of course, factual knowledge is not the only factor that matters for opinions—partisanship also matters, especially for politicized policies like the ACA (Pasek, Sood, et al. 2015; Jacobs and Mettler 2018).
2. Aalberg, Strömbäck, and De Vreese's (2012) detailed conceptual investigation argues that the "game frame" refers to coverage that is directly concerned with electoral outcomes, while the "strategy frame" describes coverage that focus on competition more generally. However, they are both part of the larger "strategic game" frame, and most researchers use these terms fairly interchangeably.
3. Although the curse of knowledge is often discussed in the same context as hindsight bias, the two are different. The curse of knowledge refers to the difficulty of taking another person's perspective on a topic that you know well, whereas hindsight bias refers to the tendency for people to claim, after an event, that they would have been able to predict it (Guilbault et al. 2004).

Chapter 4

1. In this chapter, I use the psychological conceptualization of inductive reasoning, which treats inductive reasoning as a cognitive process, rather than the philosophical approach, which understands it as a form of formal logical argument.
2. These variables were collected prior to the treatments for use as covariates.
3. A third possibility is that personal relevance encouraged people to search for information. However, there was no difference in survey completion time between the treatment and control groups, as we would expect if people in the treatment group were looking up the correct answers online.
4. The only significant predictor of answering correctly was education.
5. And this would be a very successful inductive strategy, since a pizzly bear is a grizzly-polar hybrid.
6. At the time of the survey, the Federal Reserve and Social Security held about twice as much of the debt as China and Japan.

Chapter 5

1. As Graham (2023) points out, this type of experiment cannot necessarily distinguish between "correcting misperceptions" and "reducing ignorance." However, this distinction is less important from the point of view of designing effective interventions to improve competence. What matters is the extent to which accurate information

NOTES 147

changes attitudes rather than whether, for a given person or group, that information is correcting a misperception, addressing ignorance, or (more likely), some combination of both. As Chapter 3 points out, the line between ignorance and misperception is blurry at best.
2. The plurality of content that did not fall into any of these categories were noncommittal responses like "I don't know," "no comment," and "I'm not really sure what that means."
3. Of course, many (if not most) facts can potentially be both causes and effects: a dog barking could be caused by an intruder, and that same bark could affect what that intruder does.
4. The results of this study are also published in a separate article, see Thorson and Abdelaaty (2023).
5. We recode numerical responses as correct if they are within 10 percentage points of the correct answer in either direction.

Chapter 6

1. The reliability of the measures were as follows: refugee policy ($\alpha = .67$), Social Security ($\alpha = .74$), TANF ($\alpha = .70$), and national debt policy ($\alpha = .72$)
2. To create this category I combined explicit "don't know" responses as well as responses that included only nonsense or were left blank.

Chapter 7

1. I focus here on the misperceptions that are relatively widespread. Those that were held by fewer than 20% of people were not included in the analyses in this chapter. In Study 1, this included misperceptions about Medicare (11%) and birthright citizenship (16%) (see Chapter 2 for more details). In Study 2, no misperceptions fell below this threshold.
2. Because Study 1 was conducted early on in this project, before the scope was fully identified, some of the misperceptions measured are only indirectly about existing policy. For example, the false belief that "compared to ten years ago, the percentage of Americans employed by the federal government has increased" is more of a policy *outcome* than a current policy. However, I include them in the analysis regardless because they help to answer the larger question of whether people process and retain corrections of policy-related information.
3. I employ ideology because it allows me to put political leanings on a single scale, but using party identification (i.e., R, D, and I) yields substantively similar estimates.

4. These questions were asked at the start of the "partisan interpretation" experiment described in Chapter 5.

Chapter 8

1. This number is based on a count of questions in surveys in the Roper iPoll database, and so excludes academic surveys as well as surveys not in the iPoll database.

References

Aalberg, Toril, Jesper Strömbäck, and Claes H De Vreese. 2012. "The Framing of Politics as Strategy and Game: A Review of Concepts, Operationalizations and Key Findings." *Journalism* 13 (2): 162–78.

Achen, Christopher H., and Larry M. Bartels. 2006. "It Feels Like We're Thinking: The Rationalizing Voter and Electoral Democracy." Presented at the Annual Meeting of the American Political Science Association, Philadelphia.

Achen, Christopher H., and Larry M. Bartels. 2017. *Democracy for Realists: Why Elections Do Not Produce Responsive Government*. Princeton University Press.

Allcott, Hunt, and Matthew Gentzkow. 2017. "Social Media and Fake News in the 2016 Election." *Journal of Economic Perspectives* 31 (2): 211–36.

Allen, Jennifer, Baird Howland, Markus Mobius, David Rothschild, and Duncan J. Watts. 2020. "Evaluating the Fake News Problem at the Scale of the Information Ecosystem." *Science Advances* 6 (14): eaay3539.

Althaus, Scott L. 2006. "False Starts, Dead Ends, and New Opportunities in Public Opinion Research." *Critical Review* 18 (1–3): 75–104.

Alvarez, R. Michael, and John Brehm. 2002. *Hard Choices, Easy Answers: Values, Information, and American Public Opinion*. Princeton University Press.

Amazeen, Michelle A. 2016. "Checking the Fact-Checkers in 2008: Predicting Political Ad Scrutiny and Assessing Consistency." *Journal of Political Marketing* 15 (4): 433–64.

Andersen, Kristi, and Stuart J. Thorson. 1989. "Public Discourse or Strategic Game? Changes in Our Conception of Elections." *Studies in American Political Development* 3: 262–78.

Anderson, John R. 1981. "Effects of Prior Knowledge on Memory for New Information." *Memory & Cognition* 9 (3): 237–46.

Ansolabehere, Stephen, Marc Meredith, and Erik Snowberg. 2013. "Asking About Numbers: Why and How." *Political Analysis* 21 (1): 48–69.

Arceneaux, Kevin. 2012. "Cognitive Biases and the Strength of Political Arguments." *American Journal of Political Science* 56 (2): 271–85.

Arceneaux, Kevin, and Martin Johnson. 2013. *Changing Minds or Changing Channels?: Partisan News in an Age of Choice*. University of Chicago Press.

Arceneaux, Kevin, and Ryan J. Vander Wielen. 2017. *Taming Intuition: How Reflection Minimizes Partisan Reasoning and Promotes Democratic Accountability*. Cambridge University Press.

Atkin, Charles K. 1972. "Anticipated Communication and Mass Media Information-Seeking." *Public Opinion Quarterly* 36 (2): 188–99.

Atkinson, Mary Layton. 2017. *Combative Politics: The Media and Public Perceptions of Lawmaking*. University of Chicago Press.

Atkinson, Mary Layton, John Lovett, and Frank R. Baumgartner. 2014. "Measuring the Media Agenda." *Political Communication* 31 (2): 355–80.

REFERENCES

Barabas, Jason. 2011. "Social Security Knowledge." In *Consumer Knowledge and Financial Decisions*, edited by Douglas J. Lamdin, 217–37. Springer.

Barabas, Jason, Jennifer Jerit, William Pollock, and Carlisle Rainey. 2014. "The Question(s) of Political Knowledge." *American Political Science Review* 108 (4): 840–55.

Bartels, Larry M. 2002. "Beyond the Running Tally: Partisan Bias in Political Perceptions." *Political Behavior* 24 (2): 117–50.

Bauman, Laurie J., and Elissa Greenberg Adair. 1992. "The Use of Ethnographic Interviewing to Inform Questionnaire Construction." *Health Education Quarterly* 19 (1): 9–23.

Baumgartner, Frank R., and Bryan D. Jones. 2010. *Agendas and Instability in American Politics*. University of Chicago Press.

Becker, Amy B., and Leticia Bode. 2018. "Satire as a Source for Learning? The Differential Impact of News Versus Satire Exposure on Net Neutrality Knowledge Gain." *Information, Communication & Society* 21 (4): 612–25.

Bennett, W. Lance. 1996a. "An Introduction to Journalism Norms and Representations of Politics." *Political Communication* 13 (4): 373–84.

Bennett, W. Lance. 1996b. *News: The Politics of Illusion*. Longman.

Benoit, William L., Kevin A. Stein, and Glenn J. Hansen. 2005. "*New York Times* Coverage of Presidential Campaigns." *Journalism & Mass Communication Quarterly* 82 (2): 356–76.

Berinsky, A. J. 2023. *Political Rumors*. Princeton University Press.

Berinsky, Adam. 2012. "The Birthers Are Back." YouGov.com. https://today.yougov.com/topics/politics/articles-reports/2012/02/03/birthers-are-back.

Berinsky, Adam J. 2007. "Assuming the Costs of War: Events, Elites, and American Public Support for Military Conflict." *The Journal of Politics* 69 (4): 975–97.

Berinsky, Adam J. 2017. "Rumors and Health Care Reform: Experiments in Political Misinformation." *British Journal of Political Science* 47 (2): 241–62.

Birch, Susan A. J., and Paul Bloom. 2007. "The Curse of Knowledge in Reasoning About False Beliefs." *Psychological Science* 18 (5): 382–86.

Birch, Susan A. J., Patricia E Brosseau-Liard, Taeh Haddock, and Siba E. Ghrear. 2017. "A 'Curse of Knowledge' in the Absence of Knowledge? People Misattribute Fluency When Judging How Common Knowledge Is Among Their Peers." *Cognition* 166: 447–58.

Bisanz, Jeffrey, Gay L. Bisanz, and Connie A. Korpan. 1994. "Inductive Reasoning." In *Thinking and Problem Solving*, edited by Robert J. Sternberg, 179–213. Elsevier.

Bisgaard, Martin. 2015. "Bias Will Find a Way: Economic Perceptions, Attributions of Blame, and Partisan-Motivated Reasoning During Crisis." *The Journal of Politics* 77 (3): 849–60.

Bisgaard, Martin. 2019. "How Getting the Facts Right Can Fuel Partisan-Motivated Reasoning." *American Journal of Political Science* 63 (4): 824–39.

Bode, Leticia. 2016. "Political News in the News Feed: Learning Politics from Social Media." *Mass Communication and Society* 19 (1): 24–48.

Bradburn, Norman. 2016. "How Americans Navigate the Modern Information Environment." NORC at the University of Chicago.

Bruni, Frank. 2019. "Will the Media Be Trump's Accomplice Again in 2020?" *New York Times*, January 11, 2019.

Burns, Gregory. 2022. "News Organizations Are Increasing Diversity Efforts, a Medill Survey Finds." *Poynter*. February 1, 2022. https://www.poynter.org/business-work/2022/news-media-diversity-equity-inclusion-2022/.

Callan, Mitchell J., Robbie M. Sutton, Annelie J. Harvey, and Rael J. Dawtry. 2014. "Immanent Justice Reasoning: Theory, Research, and Current Directions." In *Advances in Experimental Social Psychology*, edited by James M. Olson, Mark P. Zanna, 49:105–61. Elsevier.

Camerer, Colin, George Loewenstein, and Martin Weber. 1989. "The Curse of Knowledge in Economic Settings: An Experimental Analysis." *Journal of Political Economy* 97 (5): 1232–54.

Carey, John M., Andrew M. Guess, Peter J. Loewen, Eric Merkley, Brendan Nyhan, Joseph B. Phillips, and Jason Reifler. 2022. "The Ephemeral Effects of Fact-Checks on COVID-19 Misperceptions in the United States, Great Britain and Canada." *Nature Human Behaviour* 6 (2): 236–43.

Carlson, Matt. 2018. "Confronting Measurable Journalism." *Digital Journalism* 6 (4): 406–17.

Carlson, Taylor N. 2019. "Through the Grapevine: Informational Consequences of Interpersonal Political Communication." *American Political Science Review* 113 (2): 325–39.

Carnahan, Dustin, Daniel E. Bergan, and Sangwon Lee. 2021. "Do Corrective Effects Last? Results from a Longitudinal Experiment on Beliefs Toward Immigration in the US." *Political Behavior* 43 (3): 1227–46.

Carpentier, Francesca R. Dillman. 2008. "Applicability of the Informational Utility Model for Radio News." *Journalism & Mass Communication Quarterly* 85 (3): 577–90.

Carr, David. 2014. "Ezra Klein Is Joining Vox Media as Web Journalism Asserts Itself." *New York Times*. January 6, 2014. https://www.nytimes.com/2014/01/27/business/media/ezra-klein-joining-vox-media-as-web-journalism-asserts-itself.html.

CBS News. 2011. "CBS News Poll: Economy."

Chaffee, Steven H., and Stacey Frank Kanihan. 1997. "Learning About Politics From the Mass Media." *Political Communication* 14 (4): 421–30.

Chaffee, Steven H., and Jack M. McLeod. 1973. "Individual Vs. Social Predictors of Information Seeking." *Journalism Quarterly* 50 (2): 237–45.

Cillizza, Chris. 2015. "Trump's Ace in the Hole: Most Voters Don't Care About Policy." *Washington Post*. August 31, 2015.

CNN/ORC. 2009. "CNN/ORC Poll: Health Care Reform/Economy." Retrieved from Roper Center for Public Opinion Research.

Cohen, Tom. 2014. "5 Years Later, Here's How the Tea Party Changed Politics." CNN. February 28, 2014.

Cook, Fay Lomax, Lawrence R. Jacobs, and Dukhong Kim. 2010. "Trusting What You Know: Information, Knowledge, and Confidence in Social Security." *The Journal of Politics* 72 (2): 397–412.

Coppock, Alexander Edwards. 2023. *Persuasion in parallel: How information changes minds about politics*. University of Chicago Press.

Coppock, Alexander, and Oliver A. McClellan. 2019. "Validating the Demographic, Political, Psychological, and Experimental Results Obtained from a New Source of Online Survey Respondents." *Research & Politics* 6 (1): 2053168018822174.

Corasaniti, Nick. 2016. "A Look at Trump's Immigration Plan, Then and Now." *New York Times*. August 31, 2016. https://www.nytimes.com/interactive/2016/08/31/us/politics/donald-trump-immigration-changes.html.

Craighead, Bill. 2011. "The Wrong Budget Analogy." *Los Angeles Times*. August 24, 2011.

Cramer, Katherine J. 2016. *The Politics of Resentment: Rural Consciousness in Wisconsin and the Rise of Scott Walker*. University of Chicago Press.

Czopek, Madison. 2020. "No, Kamala Harris Didn't Say This About Guns." Politifact.com. August 17, 2020. https://www.politifact.com/factchecks/2020/aug/17/facebook-posts/no-kamala-harris-didnt-say-about-guns/.

Dafoe, Allan, Baobao Zhang, and Devin Caughey. 2018. "Information Equivalence in Survey Experiments." *Political Analysis* 26 (4): 399–416.

Davis, Alyssa. 2016. "In U.S., Concern About Crime Climbs to 15-Year High." Gallup. April 6, 2016. http://www.gallup.com/poll/190475/americans-concern-crime-climbs-year-high.aspx.

Delli Carpini, Michael, and Scott Keeter. 1996. *What Americans Know About Politics and Why It Matters*. Yale University Press.

Desimone, Laura M., and Kerstin Carlson Le Floch. 2004. "Are We Asking the Right Questions? Using Cognitive Interviews to Improve Surveys in Education Research." *Educational Evaluation and Policy Analysis* 26 (1): 1–22.

Deuze, Mark. 2005. "What Is Journalism? Professional Identity and Ideology of Journalists Reconsidered." *Journalism* 6 (4): 442–64.

DiJulio, Bianca, and Mollyann Brodie. 2016. "Americans' Views on the U.S. Role in Global Health." The Henry J. Kaiser Family Foundation. January 20, 2016. http://www.kff.org/global-health-policy/poll-finding/americans-views-on-the-u-s-role-in-global-health/.

Dolan, Kathleen. 2011. "Do Women and Men Know Different Things? Measuring Gender Differences in Political Knowledge." *The Journal of Politics* 73 (1): 97–107.

Dowling, Conor, Michael Henderson, and Michael Miller. 2020. "Knowledge Persists, Opinions Drift: Learning and Opinion Change in a Three-Wave Panel Experiment." *American Politics Research* 48 (2): 263–74.

Druckman, James N. 2014. "Pathologies of Studying Public Opinion, Political Communication, and Democratic Responsiveness." *Political Communication* 31 (3): 467–92.

Druckman, Jamie. 2022. *Experimental Thinking*. Cambridge University Press.

Economist. 2016. "The Post-Truth World—Yes, I'd Lie to You." *Economist*. September 10, 2016. https://www.economist.com/briefing/2016/09/10/yes-id-lie-to-you.

Eide, Martin, and Graham Knight. 1999. "Public/Private Service: Service Journalism and the Problems of Everyday Life." *European Journal of Communication* 14 (4): 525–47.

Evans, Geoffrey, and Robert Andersen. 2006. "The Political Conditioning of Economic Perceptions." *Journal of Politics* 68 (1): 194–207.

Evans, Geoffrey, and Mark Pickup. 2010. "Reversing the Causal Arrow: The Political Conditioning of Economic Perceptions in the 2000–2004 US Presidential Election Cycle." *The Journal of Politics* 72 (4): 1236–51.

Fallows, James M. 1997. *Breaking the News: How the Media Undermine American Democracy*. Vintage.

Faris, Robert, Hal Roberts, Bruce Etling, Nikki Bourassa, Ethan Zuckerman, and Yochai Benkler. 2017. "Partisanship, Propaganda, and Disinformation: Online Media and the 2016 US Presidential Election." Berkman Center.

Feeney, Aidan, and Evan Heit. 2007. *Inductive Reasoning: Experimental, Developmental, and Computational Approaches*. Cambridge University Press.

Ferrer-Conill, Raul, and Edson C. Tandoc Jr. 2018. "The Audience-Oriented Editor: Making Sense of the Audience in the Newsroom." *Digital Journalism* 6 (4): 436–53.

Fiorina, Morris P. 1981. "Retrospective Voting in American National Elections." Yale University Press.

Fishkin, James S. 2011. *When the People Speak: Deliberative Democracy and Public Consultation*. Oxford University Press.

Flynn, D. J., Brendan Nyhan, and Jason Reifler. 2017. "The Nature and Origins of Misperceptions: Understanding False and Unsupported Beliefs About Politics." *Political Psychology* 38 (S1): 127–50.

Forde, Kathy Roberts. 2007. "Discovering the Explanatory Report in American Newspapers." *Journalism Practice* 1 (2): 227–44.

Francovic, Kathy. 2016. "Trump Voters Perceive Greater Threats to America Than Clinton Voters." YouGov.com. September 30, 2016. https://today.yougov.com/news/2016/09/30/trump-voters-perceive-greater-threats/.

Gaines, Brian J., James H. Kuklinski, Paul J. Quirk, Buddy Peyton, and Jay Verkuilen. 2007. "Same Facts, Different Interpretations: Partisan Motivation and Opinion on Iraq." *The Journal of Politics* 69 (4): 957–74.

Gallup. 2017. "American Views: Trust, Media, and Democracy." Knight Foundation.

Gamson, William A. 1992. *Talking Politics*. Cambridge University Press.

Garrett, R. K., and B. Weeks. 2013. "The Promise and Peril of Real-Time Corrections to Political Misperceptions." Paper presented at the CSCW '13 Proceedings of the 2013 conference on Computer supported cooperative work, San Antonio, TX.

Gerber, Alan S, and Gregory A Huber. 2010. "Partisanship, Political Control, and Economic Assessments." *American Journal of Political Science* 54 (1): 153–73.

Gilardi, Fabrizio, Theresa Gessler, Maël Kubli, and Stefan Müller. 2022. "Social Media and Political Agenda Setting." *Political Communication* 39 (1): 39–60.

Gilens, Martin. 2001. "Political Ignorance and Collective Policy Preferences." *American Political Science Review* 95 (2): 379–96.

Gollust, Sarah E., Laura M. Baum, Jeff Niederdeppe, Colleen L. Barry, and Erika Franklin Fowler. 2017. "Local Television News Coverage of the Affordable Care Act: Emphasizing Politics Over Consumer Information." *American Journal of Public Health* 107 (5): 687–93.

Graham, Matthew. 2023. "Measuring Misperceptions." *American Political Science Review* 117 (1): 80–102.

Graves, Lucas. 2016. *Deciding What's True: The Rise of Political Fact-Checking in American Journalism*. Columbia University Press.

Graves, Lucas, and Alexios Mantzarlis. 2020. "Amid Political Spin and Online Misinformation, Fact Checking Adapts." *The Political Quarterly* 91 (3): 585–91.

Grigorieff, Alexis, Christopher Roth, and Diego Ubfal. 2020. "Does Information Change Attitudes Toward Immigrants?" *Demography* 57 (3): 1117–43.

Guilbault, Rebecca L, Fred B. Bryant, Jennifer Howard Brockway, and Emil J. Posavac. 2004. "A Meta-Analysis of Research on Hindsight Bias." *Basic and Applied Social Psychology* 26 (2–3): 103–17.

Hardy, Bruce W, Jeffrey A. Gottfried, Kenneth M. Winneg, and Kathleen Hall Jamieson. 2014. "Stephen Colbert's Civics Lesson: How Colbert Super PAC Taught Viewers About Campaign Finance." *Mass Communication and Society* 17 (3): 329–53.

Hayes, Brett K., and Evan Heit. 2013. "How Similar Are Recognition Memory and Inductive Reasoning?" *Memory & Cognition* 41 (5): 781–95.

Hayes, Brett K, and Evan Heit. 2018. "Inductive Reasoning 2.0." *Wiley Interdisciplinary Reviews: Cognitive Science* 9 (3): e1459.

Healy, Andrew, and Neil Malhotra. 2013. "Retrospective Voting Reconsidered." *Annual Review of Political Science* 16: 285–306.

Healy, Jack. 2014. "Senate Seat of Baucus Is Filled in Montana." *New York Times*. February 7, 2014. https://www.nytimes.com/2014/02/08/us/politics/montana-governor-names-replacement-for-baucus.html.

Hilton, Denis. 2017. "Social Attribution and Explanation." In *The Oxford Handbook of Causal Reasoning*, edited by M. R. Waldmann, 645–76. Oxford University Press.

Ho, Benjamin, and Peng Liu. 2015. "Herd Journalism: Investment in Novelty and Popularity in Markets for News." *Information Economics and Policy* 31: 33–46.

Hochschild, Jennifer L., and Katherine Levine Einstein. 2015. "Do Facts Matter? Information and Misinformation in American Politics." *Political Science Quarterly* 130 (4): 585–624.

Holbrook, Allyson L., Matthew K Berent, Jon A. Krosnick, Penny S. Visser, and David S. Boninger. 2005. "Attitude Importance and the Accumulation of Attitude-Relevant Knowledge in Memory." *Journal of Personality and Social Psychology* 88 (5): 749.

Hollander, Barry A. 2010. "Persistence in the Perception of Barack Obama as a Muslim in the 2008 Presidential Campaign." *Journal of Media and Religion* 9 (2): 55–66.

Hopkins, Daniel J., John Sides, and Jack Citrin. 2019. "The Muted Consequences of Correct Information About Immigration." *The Journal of Politics* 81 (1): 315–20.

Howell, William, Martin West, and Paul E. Peterson. 2011. "Meeting of the Minds." *Education Next* 11 (1): 20–31.

Iyengar, Shanto. 1994. *Is Anyone Responsible?: How Television Frames Political Issues*. University of Chicago Press.

Iyengar, Shanto, Helmut Norpoth, and Kyu S. Hahn. 2004. "Consumer Demand for Election News: The Horserace Sells." *Journal of Politics* 66 (1): 157–75.

Jacobs, Lawrence R., and Suzanne Mettler. 2018. "When and How New Policy Creates New Politics: Examining the Feedback Effects of the Affordable Care Act on Public Opinion." *Perspectives on Politics* 16 (2): 345–63.

Jacobson, Louis. 2017. "Donald Trump Wrong That Murder Rate Is Highest in 47 Years." PolitiFact. February 8, 2017. http://www.politifact.com/truth-o-meter/statements/2017/feb/08/donald-trump/donald-trump-wrong-murder-rate-highest-47-years/.

Jang, S. Mo, and Yu Won Oh. 2016. "Getting Attention Online in Election Coverage: Audience Selectivity in the 2012 US Presidential Election." *New Media & Society* 18 (10): 2271–86.

Jennings, M. Kent. 1996. "Political Knowledge Over Time and Across Generations." *Public Opinion Quarterly* 60 (2): 228–52.

Jerit, Jennifer. 2009. "Understanding the Knowledge Gap: The Role of Experts and Journalists." *The Journal of Politics* 71 (2): 442–56.

Jerit, J., and J. Barabas. 2006. "Bankrupt Rhetoric: How Misleading Information Affects Knowledge about Social Security." *Public Opinion Quarterly* 70 (3): 278–303.

Jones, Jeffrey. 2019. "New High in US Say Immigration Most Important Problem." Gallup. June 21, 2019. https://news.gallup.com/poll/259103/new-high-say-immigration-important-problem.aspx.

Jørgensen, F., and Osmundsen, M. 2022. "Correcting Citizens' Misperceptions about non-Western Immigrants: Corrective Information, Interpretations, and Policy Opinions." *Journal of Experimental Political Science*, 9(1), 64–73.

Kahan, Dan M. 2015. "Climate-Science Communication and the Measurement Problem." *Political Psychology* 36: 1–43.

Kahan, Dan M., Ellen Peters, Erica Cantrell Dawson, and Paul Slovic. 2017. "Motivated Numeracy and Enlightened Self-Government." *Behavioural Public Policy* 1 (1): 54–86.

Kahneman, D. 2011. *Thinking, Fast and Slow*. Macmillan.

Kaplan, Kalman J., and Martin Fishbein. 1969. "The Source of Beliefs, Their Saliency, and Prediction of Attitude." *The Journal of Social Psychology* 78 (1): 63–74.

Kaye, Barbara K., and Thomas J. Johnson. 2002. "Online and in the Know: Uses and Gratifications of the Web for Political Information." *Journal of Broadcasting & Electronic Media* 46 (1): 54–71.

Keane, Erin. 2016. "From Truthiness to Post-Truth, Just in Time for Donald Trump: Oxford Dictionaries' Word of the Year Should Scare the Hell Out of You." *Salon*. November 19, 2016. https://www.salon.com/2016/11/19/from-truthiness-to-post-truth-just-in-time-for-donald-trump-oxford-dictionaries-word-of-the-year-should-scare-the-hell-out-of-you/.

Kim, Jin Woo, and Eunji Kim. 2019. "Identifying the Effect of Political Rumor Diffusion Using Variations in Survey Timing." *Quarterly Journal of Political Science* 14 (3): 293–311.

Klar, Samara, and Yanna Krupnikov. 2016. *Independent Politics*. Cambridge University Press.

Klašnja, Marko, Pablo Barberá, Nicholas Beauchamp, Jonathan Nagler, and Joshua A Tucker. 2015. "Measuring Public Opinion With Social Media Data." In *The Oxford Handbook of Polling and Polling Methods*, edited by Lonna Rae Atkeson and R. Michael Alvarez, 555–82. Oxford University Press.

Knobe, Joshua. 2004. "Intention, Intentional Action and Moral Considerations." *Analysis* 64 (2): 181–87.

Knobloch, Silvia, Francesca Dillman Carpentier, and Dolf Zillmann. 2003. "Effects of Salience Dimensions of Informational Utility on Selective Exposure to Online News." *Journalism & Mass Communication Quarterly* 80 (1): 91–108.

Knobloch-Westerwick, Silvia. 2014. *Choice and Preference in Media Use: Advances in Selective Exposure Theory and Research*. Routledge.

Knobloch-Westerwick, Silvia, Francesca Dilltnan Carpentier, Andree Blumhoff, and Nico Nickel. 2005. "Selective Exposure Effects for Positive and Negative News: Testing the Robustness of the Informational Utility Model." *Journalism & Mass Communication Quarterly* 82 (1): 181–95.

Koning, Els de, Jo H. M. Hamers, Klaas Sijtsma, and Adri Vermeer. 2002. "Teaching Inductive Reasoning in Primary Education." *Developmental Review* 22 (2): 211–41.

Krawczyk, Daniel. 2017. *Reasoning: The Neuroscience of How We Think*. Elsevier.

Krugman, Paul. 2012. "Nobody Understands Debt." *New York Times*. January 1, 2012.

Kuklinski, James H., and Paul J. Quirk. 2001. "Conceptual Foundations of Citizen Competence." *Political Behavior* 23 (3): 285–311.

Kuklinski, James H., Paul J. Quirk, Jennifer Jerit, and Robert F. Rich. 2001. "The Political Environment and Citizen Competence." *American Journal of Political Science* 45 (2): 410–24.

Kuklinski, J., P. Quirk, D. Schweider, and R. F. Rich. 2000. "Misinformation and the Currency of Democratic Citizenship." *Journal of Politics* 623: 790–816.

Landler, Marc, and Richard Oppel. 2012. "Obama and Ryan Trade Blasts Over Medicare at AARP Convention." *New York Times*. September 21, 2012. https://www.nytimes.com/2012/09/22/us/politics/medicare-takes-center-stage-on-the-campaign-trail.html.

Lau, Richard R., and David P Redlawsk. 2001. "Advantages and Disadvantages of Cognitive Heuristics in Political Decision Making." *American Journal of Political Science*, 45(4): 951–71.

Lawrence, E. D., and J. Sides. 2014. "The Consequences of Political Innumeracy." *Research and Politics* 1 (2).

Lawrence, Regina G. 2000. "Game-Framing the Issues: Tracking the Strategy Frame in Public Policy News." *Political Communication* 17 (2): 93–114.

Lazer, David M. J., Matthew A. Baum, Yochai Benkler, Adam J. Berinsky, Kelly M. Greenhill, Filippo Menczer, Miriam J. Metzger, Brendan Nyhan, Gordon Pennycook, David Rothschild, Michael Schudson, Steven A. Sloman, Cass R. Sunstein, Emily A. Thorson, Duncan J. Watts, And Jonathan L. Zittrain. 2018. "The Science of Fake News." *Science* 359 (6380): 1094–96.

Lippmann, Walter. 1922. *Public Opinion*. Transaction.

Lodge, Milton, and Charles S. Taber. 2013. *The Rationalizing Voter*. Cambridge University Press.

Lupia, Arthur. 2006. "How Elitism Undermines the Study of Voter Competence." *Critical Review* 18 (1–3): 217–32.

Lupia, Arthur. 2015. *Uninformed: Why People Seem to Know So Little About Politics and What We Can Do About It*. Oxford University Press.

Lupia, Arthur, Mathew D. McCubbins, et al. 1998. *The Democratic Dilemma: Can Citizens Learn What They Need to Know?* Cambridge University Press.

Luskin, Robert C., and John G Bullock. 2011. "'Don't Know' Means 'Don't Know': DK Responses and the Public's Level of Political Knowledge." *The Journal of Politics* 73 (2): 547–57.

Mansbridge, Jane J. 1983. *Beyond Adversary Democracy*. University of Chicago Press.

McCombs, Maxwell E., and Donald L. Shaw. 1972. "The Agenda-Setting Function of Mass Media." *Public Opinion Quarterly* 36 (2): 176–87.

McCright, Aaron M., and Riley E. Dunlap. 2011. "The Politicization of Climate Change and Polarization in the American Public's Views of Global Warming, 2001–2010." *The Sociological Quarterly* 52 (2): 155–94.

McGregor, Shannon, and Daniel Kreiss. 2020. "Americans Are Too Worried About Political Misinformation." Slate. October 30, 2020. https://slate.com/technology/2020/10/misinformation-social-media-election-research-fear.html.

Mercado, Dana. 2018. "What You Don't Know About Medicare Can Cost You." CNBC. June 27, 2018. https://www.cnbc.com/2018/06/27/threekey-facts-youre-getting-wrong-about-medicare.html.

Mettler, Suzanne. 2011. *The Submerged State: How Invisible Government Policies Undermine American Democracy*. University of Chicago Press.

Miller, Joanne M., Kyle L. Saunders, and Christina E. Farhart. 2016. "Conspiracy Endorsement as Motivated Reasoning: The Moderating Roles of Political Knowledge and Trust." *American Journal of Political Science* 60 (4): 824–44.

Miroff, Nick. 2020. "Trump Cuts Refugee Cap to Lowest Level Ever, Depicts Them on Campaign Trail as a Threat and Burden." *Washington Post*. October 1, 2020.

Moses, Lucia. 2014. "*The New York Times* Explains Its New Explainer Site." Digiday. April 21, 2014. https://digiday.com/media/new-york-times-explains-upshot/.

Mummolo, Jonathan. 2016. "News From the Other Side: How Topic Relevance Limits the Prevalence of Partisan Selective Exposure." *The Journal of Politics* 78 (3): 763–73.

Mutz, Diana. 2011. *Population-Based Survey Experiments*. Cambridge University Press.

Mutz, Diana C. 1993. "Direct and Indirect Routes to Politicizing Personal Experience: Does Knowledge Make A Difference?" *Public Opinion Quarterly* 57 (4): 483–502.

Nadeau, Richard, and Richard G. Niemi. 1995. "Educated Guesses: The Process of Answering Factual Knowledge Questions in Surveys." *Public Opinion Quarterly* 59 (3): 323–46.

Norris, Floyd. 2014. "A Dire Economic Forecast Based on New Assumptions." *New York Times*. February 27, 2014.

Nyhan, Brendan. 2010. "Why the 'Death Panel' Myth Wouldn't Die: Misinformation in the Health Care Reform Debate." *Politics* 8 (1): 5.

Nyhan, Brendan. 2020. "Facts and Myths About Misperceptions." *Journal of Economic Perspectives* 34 (3): 220–36.

Nyhan, Brendan. 2021. "Why the Backfire Effect Does Not Explain the Durability of Political Misperceptions." *Proceedings of the National Academy of Sciences* 118 (15).

Nyhan, Brendan, Ethan Porter, Jason Reifler, and Thomas J. Wood. 2019. "Taking Fact-Checks Literally but Not Seriously? The Effects of Journalistic Fact-Checking on Factual Beliefs and Candidate Favorability." *Political Behavior*, 1–22.

Nyhan, B., and J. Reifler. 2010. "When Corrections Fail: The Persistence of Political Misperceptions." *Political Behavior* 32: 202–330.

OECD. 2016. "OECD International Aid."

Olsen, Asmus Leth. 2017. "Compared to What: How Social and Historical Reference Points Affect Citizens' Performance Evaluations." *Journal of Public Administration Research and Theory* 27 (4): 562–80.

Osherson, Daniel N., Edward E. Smith, Ormond Wilkie, Alejandro Lopez, and Eldar Shafir. 1990. "Category-Based Induction." *Psychological Review* 97 (2): 185.

Page, B. I., and R. Y. Shapiro. 2010. *The Rational Public: Fifty Years of Trends in Americans' Policy Preferences*. University of Chicago Press.

Pasek, Josh, and Jon Krosnick. 2010. "Optimizing Survey Questionnaire Design in Political Science: Insights from Psychology." In *The Oxford Handbook of American Elections and Political Behavior*, edited by Jan E. Leighley. Oxford University Press.

Pasek, Josh, Gaurav Sood, and Jon Krosnick. 2015. "Misinformed About the Affordable Care Act? Leveraging Certainty to Assess the Prevalence of Misperceptions." *Journal of Communication* 65 (4): 660–73.

Pasek, Josh, Tobias H. Stark, Jon A. Krosnick, and Trevor Tompson. 2015. "What Motivates a Conspiracy Theory? Birther Beliefs, Partisanship, Liberal-Conservative Ideology, and Anti-Black Attitudes." *Electoral Studies* 40: 482–89.

Patterson, Thomas E. 2011. *Out of Order: An Incisive and Boldly Original Critique of the News Media's Domination of Ameri*. Vintage.

Patterson, Thomas E. 2013. *Informing the News*. Vintage.

Patterson, Thomas E. 2016. "News Coverage of the 2016 General Election: How the Press Failed the Voters." Shorenstein Center on Media, Politics and Public Policy.

Peter G. Peterson Foundation. 2019. "Peterson Fiscal Confidence Index Poll." www.pjfp.org. https://www.pgpf.org/what-we-are-doing/education-and-awareness/fiscal-confidence-index.

Petersen, Michael Bang, and Lene Aaroe. 2013. "Politics in the Mind's Eye: Imagination as a Link Between Social and Political Cognition." *American Political Science Review* 107 (2): 275–93.

Pew Research Center. 2017. "Vast Majority of Americans Say Benefits of Childhood Vaccines Outweigh Risks." PewResearch.org. https://www.pewresearch.org/science/

2017/02/02/vast-majority-of-americans-say-benefits-of-childhood-vaccines-outweigh-risks/.

Pinker, Steven. 2014. "The Source of Bad Writing." *Wall Street Journal*. September 25, 2014.

Politifact. 2017. "The Principles of PolitiFact, PunditFact and the Truth-o-Meter." http://www.politifact.com/truth-o-meter/article/2013/nov/01/principles-politifact-punditfact-and-truth-o-meter/.

Porter, Ethan, and Thomas J. Wood. 2019. *False Alarm: The Truth About Political Mistruths in the Trump Era*. Cambridge University Press.

Porter, Ethan, Thomas J. Wood, and Babak Bahador. 2019. "Can Presidential Misinformation on Climate Change Be Corrected? Evidence from Internet and Phone Experiments." *Research & Politics* 6 (3): 2053168019864784.

Porter, William C., and Flint Stephens. 1989. "Estimating Readability: A Study of Utah Editors' Abilities." *Newspaper Research Journal* 10 (2): 87–96.

Prior, Markus. 2007. *Post-Broadcast Democracy: How Media Choice Increases Inequality in Political Involvement and Polarizes Elections*. Cambridge University Press.

Prior, Markus. 2018. *Hooked: How Politics Captures People's Interest*. Cambridge University Press.

Prior, Markus, Gaurav Sood, Kabir Khanna, et al. 2015. "You Cannot Be Serious: The Impact of Accuracy Incentives on Partisan Bias in Reports of Economic Perceptions." *Quarterly Journal of Political Science* 10 (4): 489–518.

Ramo, Danielle E., Sharon M. Hall, and Judith J. Prochaska. 2010. "Reaching Young Adult Smokers Through the Internet: Comparison of Three Recruitment Mechanisms." *Nicotine & Tobacco Research*, ntq086.

Rehder, Bob, and Michael R. Waldmann. 2017. "Failures of Explaining Away and Screening Off in Described Versus Experienced Causal Learning Scenarios." *Memory & Cognition* 45 (2): 245–60.

Rich, Patrick R., and Maria S. Zaragoza. 2016. "The Continued Influence of Implied and Explicitly Stated Misinformation in News Reports." *Journal of Experimental Psychology: Learning, Memory, and Cognition* 42 (1): 62.

Robbett, Andrew, and Peter Hans Matthews. 2020. "Democrats and Republicans Disagree About Covid-19 Facts." Nieman Lab. August 31, 2020. https://www.niemanlab.org/2020/08/democrats-and-republicans-disagree-about-covid-19-facts-in-a-divide-that-goes-beyond-usual-political-partisanship/.

Roberts, David. 2019. "My Advice for Aspiring Explainer Journalists." Vox.com. October 25, 2019.

Robertson, Lori. 2021. "Cheney's Misleading Criticism of the COVID-19 Relief Package." FactCheck.org. March 12, 2021. https://www.factcheck.org/2021/03/cheneys-misleading-criticism-of-the-covid-19-relief-package/.

Robison, Joshua. 2014. "Who Knows? Question Format and Political Knowledge." *International Journal of Public Opinion Research* 27 (1): 1–21.

Rosset, Evelyn. 2008. "It's No Accident: Our Bias for Intentional Explanations." *Cognition* 108 (3): 771–80.

Rucker, Philip. 2009. "Sen. DeMint of S.C. Is Voice of Opposition to Health-Care Reform." *NBC News*. July 28, 2019.

Ruggiero, Thomas E. 2000. "Uses and Gratifications Theory in the 21st Century." *Mass Communication & Society* 3 (1): 3–37.

Saad, Lydia. 2015. "Cluster of Concerns Vie for Top U.S. Problem in 2014." Gallup. January 2, 2015. https://news.gallup.com/poll/180398/cluster-concerns-vie-top-problem-2014.aspx.

Schaffner, Brian F., and Samantha Luks. 2018. "Misinformation or Expressive Responding? What an Inauguration Crowd Can Tell Us About the Source of Political Misinformation in Surveys." *Public Opinion Quarterly* 82 (1): 135–47.

Schmidt, Andreas, Ana Ivanova, and Mike S. Schäfer. 2013. "Media Attention for Climate Change Around the World: A Comparative Analysis of Newspaper Coverage in 27 Countries." *Global Environmental Change* 23 (5): 1233–48.

Schneider, Saundra K., and William G. Jacoby. 2005. "Elite Discourse and American Public Opinion: The Case of Welfare Spending." *Political Research Quarterly* 58 (3): 367–79.

Schuman, Howard, and Stanley Presser. 1996. *Questions and Answers in Attitude Surveys: Experiments on Question Form, Wording, and Context*. SAGE.

Scotto, Thomas J., Jason Reifler, David Hudson, and Jennifer van Heerde-Hudson. 2017. "We Spend How Much? Misperceptions, Innumeracy, and Support for the Foreign Aid in the United States and Great Britain." *Journal of Experimental Political Science* 4 (2): 119–28.

Scribner, Todd. 2017. "You Are Not Welcome Here Anymore: Restoring Support for Refugee Resettlement in the Age of Trump." *Journal on Migration and Human Security* 5 (2): 263–84.

Searles, Kathleen, Martha Humphries Ginn, and Jonathan Nickens. 2016. "For Whom the Poll Airs: Comparing Poll Results to Television Poll Coverage." *Public Opinion Quarterly* 80 (4): 943–63.

Sharon, Aviv J., and Ayelet Baram-Tsabari. 2014. "Measuring Mumbo Jumbo: A Preliminary Quantification of the Use of Jargon in Science Communication." *Public Understanding of Science* 23 (5): 528–46.

Shatz, Itamar. 2022. "The Curse of Knowledge When Teaching Statistics." *Teaching Statistics* 45 (2023): 22–26.

Shear, Michael, and Zolan Kanno-Youngs. 2019. "Trump Slashes Refugee Cap to 18,000, Curtailing U.S. Role as Haven." *New York Times*. September 26, 2019. https://www.nytimes.com/2019/09/26/us/politics/trump-refugees.html.

Shepardson, David. 2017. "Trump Administration to Propose 'Dramatic Reductions' in Foreign Aid." Reuters. March 4, 2017. https://www.reuters.com/article/us-usa-budget-idUSKBN16B0NC.

Shesgreen, Deirdre. 2020. "Trump Administration Slashes Refugee Program Amid President's Campaign Attacks on Immigrants." *USA Today*. October 1, 2020.

Shoemaker, Pamela J. 1996. "Hardwired for News: Using Biological and Cultural Evolution to Explain the Surveillance Function." *Journal of Communication* 46 (3): 32–47.

Sides, John. 2016. "Stories or Science? Facts, Frames, and Policy Attitudes." *American Politics Research* 44 (3): 387–414.

Sides, John, Michael Tesler, and Lynn Vavreck. 2019. *Identity Crisis: The 2016 Presidential Campaign and the Battle for the Meaning of America*. Princeton University Press.

Sigelman, Lee, and David Bullock. 1991. "Candidates, Issues, Horse Races, and Hoopla: Presidential Campaign Coverage, 1888–1988." *American Politics Quarterly* 19 (1): 5–32.

Silverman, Craig. 2016. "This Analysis Shows How Fake Election News Stories Outperformed Real News on Facebook." Buzzfeed News. November 16, 2016.

Sloman, Steven A., and David Lagnado. 2015. "Causality in Thought." *Annual Review of Psychology* 66: 223–47.

Sloman, Steven, and Philip Fernbach. 2018. *The Knowledge Illusion: Why We Never Think Alone*. Penguin.

Soroka, Stuart N. 2002. "Issue Attributes and Agenda-Setting by Media, the Public, and Policymakers in Canada." *International Journal of Public Opinion Research* 14 (3): 264–85.

Soroka, Stuart N., and Christopher Wlezien. 2022. *Information and Democracy*. Cambridge University Press.

Southwell, Brian G., Emily A. Thorson, and Laura Sheble. 2018. *Misinformation and Mass Audiences*. University of Texas Press.

Steenkamp, Jan-Benedict, and Hans Van Trijp. 1997. "Attribute Elicitation in Marketing Research: A Comparison of Three Procedures." *Marketing Letters* 8 (2): 153–65.

Sturgis, Patrick, Nick Allum, and Patten Smith. 2007. "An Experiment on the Measurement of Political Knowledge in Surveys." *Public Opinion Quarterly* 72 (1): 90–102.

Sullivan, Margaret. 2019. "Campaign Journalism Needs an Overhaul. Here's One Radical Idea." *Washington Post*.

Swire, Briony, Adam J. Berinsky, Stephan Lewandowsky, and Ullrich K. H. Ecker. 2017. "Processing Political Misinformation: Comprehending the Trump Phenomenon." *Royal Society Open Science* 4 (3): 160802.

Swire, Briony, and Ullrich K. H. Ecker. 2018. "Misinformation and Its Correction: Cognitive Mechanisms and Recommendations for Mass Communication." In *Misinformation and Mass Audiences*, edited by B. Southwell, E. Thorson, and L. Sheble, 195–211.

Taleb, Nassim. 2005. *Fooled by Randomness: The Hidden Role of Chance in Life and in the Markets*. Vol. 1. Random House.

Talericao, Kate. 2018. "Idaho Supreme Court Will Hear Challenge to Medicaid Expansion." *The Spokesman-Review*. December 4, 2018. http://www.spokesman.com/stories/2018/dec/04/idaho-supreme-court-will-hear-challenge-to-medicai/.

Thorson, Emily. 2016. "Belief Echoes: The Persistent Effects of Corrected Misinformation." *Political Communication* 33 (3): 460–80.

Thorson, Emily, and Lamis Abdelaaty. 2023. "Misperceptions About Refugee Policy." *American Political Science Review* 117 (3): 1123–9.

Tilley, James, and Sara B Hobolt. 2011. "Is the Government to Blame? An Experimental Test of How Partisanship Shapes Perceptions of Performance and Responsibility." *The Journal of Politics* 73 (2): 316–30.

Timms, Jane. 2016. "Fact-Checking Donald Trump's Immigration Speech in Arizona." *NBC News*. September 1, 2016.

Toff, Benjamin, and Antonis Kalogeropoulos. 2020. "All the News That's Fit to Ignore: How the Information Environment Does and Does Not Shape News Avoidance." *Public Opinion Quarterly* 84 (S1): 366–90.

Trussler, Marc, and Stuart Soroka. 2014. "Consumer Demand for Cynical and Negative News Frames." *The International Journal of Press/Politics* 19 (3): 360–79.

Udani, Adriano. 2018. "Inferring What Hardliners Would Do: Assessing Factual Knowledge of State Policies on Immigrant Treatment in the US." *Politics, Groups, and Identities* 6 (4): 631–49.

Usher, Nikki. 2012. "Service Journalism as Community Experience: Personal Technology and Personal Finance at the *New York Times*." *Journalism Practice* 6 (1): 107–21.

Usher, Nikki. 2021. *News for the Rich, White, and Blue: How Place and Power Distort American Journalism.* Columbia University Press.

Van Erkel, Patrick F. A., and Peter Van Aelst. 2021. "Why Don't We Learn From Social Media? Studying Effects of and Mechanisms Behind Social Media News Use on General Surveillance Political Knowledge." *Political Communication* 38 (4): 407–25.

Van Ittersum, Koert, Joost M. E. Pennings, Brian Wansink, and Hans C. M. Van Trijp. 2007. "The Validity of Attribute-Importance Measurement: A Review." *Journal of Business Research* 60 (11): 1177–90.

Van Susteren, Greta. 2014. "Tornadoes Slamming the South." *Fox on the Record with Greta Van Susteren.*

Walsh, Katherine Cramer. 2004. *Talking About Politics: Informal Groups and Social Identity in American Life.* University of Chicago Press.

Wasike, Ben. 2018. "Preaching to the Choir? An Analysis of Newspaper Readability Vis-à-Vis Public Literacy." *Journalism* 19 (11): 1570–87.

Weeks, B. E., and R. K. Garrett. 2014. "Electoral Consequences of Political Rumors: Motivated Reasoning, Candidate Rumors, and Vote Choice During the 2008 US Presidential Election." *International Journal of Public Opinion Research* 26 (4): 401–22.

Weeks, B., and B. Southwell. 2010. "The Symbiosis of News Coverage and Aggregate Online Search Behavior: Obama, Rumors, and Presidential Politics." *Mass Communication and Society* 13 (4): 341–60.

White, Peter A. 2006. "The Causal Asymmetry." *Psychological Review* 113 (1): 132.

Whyman, Michelle C. 2018. "The Roots of Legislative Durability: How Information, Deliberation, and Compromise Create Laws That Last." PhD thesis, University of Texas.

Williamson, Scott. 2020. "Countering Misperceptions to Reduce Prejudice: An Experiment on Attitudes Toward Muslim Americans." *Journal of Experimental Political Science* 7 (3): 167–78.

Wilner, Tamar. 2016. "When It Comes to Fact-Checking, Why Do Politicians Get All the Attention." Poynter. November 7, 2016. https://www.poynter.org/fact-checking/2016/when-it-comes-to-fact-checking-why-do-politicians-get-all-the-attention/.

Wlezien, Christopher. 1995. "The Public as Thermostat: Dynamics of Preferences for Spending." *American Journal of Political Science* 39: 981–1000.

Wood, Thomas, and Ethan Porter. 2019. "The Elusive Backfire Effect: Mass Attitudes' Steadfast Factual Adherence." *Political Behavior* 41 (1): 135–63.

Worthen, Meredith G. F. 2014. "An Invitation to Use Craigslist Ads to Recruit Respondents from Stigmatized Groups for Qualitative Interviews." *Qualitative Research* 14 (3): 371–83.

Wyer, Robert S., and Dolores Albarracín. 2005. "Belief Formation, Organization, and Change: Cognitive and Motivational Influences." *The Handbook of Attitudes* 273: 322.

Xenos, Michael A., and Amy B. Becker. 2009. "Moments of Zen: Effects of the Daily Show on Information Seeking and Political Learning." *Political Communication* 26 (3): 317–32.

Zaller, John. 2003. "A New Standard of News Quality: Burglar Alarms for the Monitorial Citizen." *Political Communication* 20 (2): 109–30.

Zaller, John, and Stanley Feldman. 1992. "A Simple Theory of the Survey Response: Answering Questions Versus Revealing Preferences." *American Journal of Political Science* 36 (3): 579–616.

Index

For the benefit of digital users, indexed terms that span two pages (e.g., 52–53) may, on occasion, appear on only one of those pages.

Note: Tables and figures are indicated by *t* and *f* following the page number

Achen, Christopher H., 4, 5–6
acquiescence bias, 27–29, 121–22
Affordable Care Act (ACA) misperceptions
    confidence measures of, 29
    interpretation of policy information about, 89
    media coverage and, 38–39, 39*t*, 40–41, 42, 46–47, 48–49
    origins of, 10, 14–15, 17–18, 17*f*
    preferences distorted by, 9–10
    prevalence of, 29–31, 30*f*
agenda-setting, media coverage and, 72–74
Althaus, Scott L., 2
American National Election Survey (ANES), 8, 30–31
American Rescue Plan, 142–43
approval. *See* policy approval and priorities, effect of policy-current information on
Arceneaux, Kevin, 4
Associated Press
    coverage of national debt, 50–54, 53*t*
    policy gaps in coverage by, 43–45, 45*f*
Atkinson, Mary Layton, 38
attitudes, political
    attitudinal effects of policy facts, 92–97, 93*f*, 95*t*, 96*f*, 133–34
    difficulties of establishing causality about, 75–76, 97, 136
    facts versus, 19–20
    focus on, 136–37
    information-processing theory and, 79–81
    partisan implications of policy facts, 81–92, 83*t*, 84*f*, 85*f*, 87*t*, 97, 133–34
    studies examining correction effects on, 77–79, 78*t*
    See also corrections and corrective interventions; policy approval and priorities, effect of policy-current information on
autism and vaccines, misperceptions about, 17–18, 17*f*
availability heuristic, 15–16, 18

Barabas, Jason, 55
Bartels, Larry M., 4, 5–6
Baumgartner, Frank R., 38
Bell, Melissa, 139–40
Bennett, W. Lance., 49
bias
    acquiescence, 27–29, 121–22
    misperceptions arising from, 11, 15–16
    novelty, 36–37, 47–49, 54, 120–21
    See also partisanship and partisan identity
Biden, Joe, 42
Bisgaard, Martin, 40–41, 80, 89
Bruni, Frank, 37–38
Bush, George, 7

candidate-centered misperceptions, 6–8
Carlson, T. N., 80–81
Carpentier, Francesca Dillman, 59
causal asymmetry, 90–91
causal inference, 86–87, 87*t*, 90–91
    See also inductive reasoning
CBS, coverage of national debt, 50–54, 53*t*

charitable contributions,
    deductibility of, 49
Cheney, Liz, 143
China, U.S. debt owned by. *See* national
    debt misperceptions
Clinton, Hillary, 7, 39–40, 75
CNN, coverage of national debt, 50–54, 53*t*
cognitive bias. *See* bias
comedy, political, 143–44
Comparative Congressional Election
    Survey (CCES), 121–22
competence, effect of policy-current
    information on
    actions going forward, 134–38
    discussion of, 114–15
    misperceptions measured, 101–2, 103*t*
    overview of, 98–99
    policy accuracy, 109–10, 109*f*
    policy approval, 102, 110–11, 110*f*
    policy opinions, 111–14, 111*f*, 113*t*
    policy priorities, 102–8, 112*t*
    study design, 100–1
    study goals, 99–100
competence, threats to
    candidate-centered misperceptions, 6–8
    policy misperceptions, 8–10
    problematic versus nonproblematic
        misconceptions, 2–3
confidence measures
    assessment of, 29–30, 29*f*, 31, 32*f*
    correctability and, 125–27, 125*t*
constructed beliefs. *See* inductive
    reasoning
contestation of policy facts, 86, 87*t*, 89–90
contextual fact-checking, 130–31, 130*f*
Cooperative Congressional Election Study
    (CCES), 26–27
corrections and corrective interventions
    attitudinal effects of policy facts, 92–97,
        93*f*, 95*t*, 96*f*, 133–34
    contextual fact-checking, 130–31, 130*f*
    design of, 139–44
    difficulties of establishing causality
        about, 75–76, 97, 136
    effectiveness of, 13, 121–27, 122*t*,
        124*f*, 125*t*
    goals of, 116–17
    information-processing theory and, 79–81

partisan implications of policy facts,
    81–92, 83*t*, 84*f*, 85*f*, 87*t*, 97, 133–34
policy-current coverage, public
    appetite for, 127–29, 128*f*, 129*t*, 131–
    32, 137–38
potential barriers to, 117–21, 131, 134
static-policy, 121–23, 122*t*
studies examining effects of, 77–79, 78*t*
See also policy approval and
    priorities, effect of policy-current
    information on
COVID-19 pandemic, 4, 34–35, 94
Craigslist, recruitment of participants
    from, 20–21, 21*t*
Cramer, Katherine J., 19–20, 135
curse of knowledge, 36–37, 49–50

death panels in Affordable Care Act.
    See Affordable Care Act (ACA)
    misperceptions
Deferred Action for Childhood Arrivals
    (DACA), 42
Demaio, Carl, 53
democratic functioning, misperceptions
    in, 1–2
Democratic partisanship. *See* partisanship
    and partisan identity
dismantling of invented state, 13
    contextual fact-checking in practice,
        130–31, 130*f*
    goals of, 116–17
    integration of policy-current
        information into media
        coverage, 139–44
    potential barriers to, 117–21, 134
    See also corrections and corrective
        interventions; identification of
        misperceptions

economy, misperceptions about, 3, 4,
    75, 79, 91
education levels, impact of
    on confidence measures, 31
    on correctability, 125–27, 125*t*
    in inductive reasoning, 63, 64*t*, 70
    on partisan interpretation of facts, 84*f*
    on policy approval, accuracy, and
        priorities, 109*f*, 110*f*, 111*f*

education policy
   media coverage of, 39t
   partisan interpretation of, 81–92, 83t, 84f, 85f, 87t, 97, 133–34
entitlement program misperceptions
   inductive reasoning leading to, 67–69, 68t
   issue relevance and inductive reasoning, 60–66, 62f, 64t
   partisanship and, 33, 33t, 81–92, 83t, 84f, 85f, 87t
   prevalence of, 29–31, 29f, 30f
   scope of, 26–29, 28t
   See also identification of misperceptions; Social Security misperceptions; TANF policy misconceptions
environment policy, partisanship and, 81–92, 83t, 84f, 85f, 87t
evaluation of policy facts, 86, 87t, 89
explainer journalism, 139–40, 144
explaining away, 91

fact-checking organizations, 15, 16
"fake news"
   academic focus on, 137
   dissemination of, 55
   identification of, 135
   misperceptions created by, 7, 14–15, 17–18, 34, 56–57, 134–35
   political interest and, 32
Feldman, Stanley, 64–65, 74
Flynn, D. J., 31
folk wisdom, beliefs shaped by, 4
food stamp policy misconceptions
   correction of, 123–27, 124f, 125t
   partisanship and, 81–92, 83t, 84f, 85f, 87t
   prevalence of, 122t, 122–23
   See also TANF policy misconceptions
foreign aid misperceptions, 15–16, 17–18, 17f
FOX, coverage of national debt, 50–54, 53t
frames, strategy, 36–37, 46–47

Gaines, Brian J., 79–80
game frames, 36–37, 46–47, 52–54
Gamson, William, 19–20
gender, political knowledge and, 32–33, 63
Gollust, Sarah E., 47

government size misconceptions
   correction of, 123–27, 124f, 125t
   identification of (*see* identification of misperceptions)
   partisanship and, 33, 33t
   prevalence of, 29–31, 30f
Great Depression, 49

Harris, Kamala, 118–19
Hart-Celler Act, 49
HealthCare.gov, 47
healthcare policy
   media coverage of, 39t
   partisanship and, 4, 81–92, 83t, 84f, 85f, 87t
   See also Affordable Care Act (ACA) misperceptions
Hurricane Katrina misconceptions, 29–31, 30f

identification of misperceptions
   confidence measures, 29–30, 29f, 31, 32f
   interviews, 19–26, 34–35, 142–43
   kinds of people holding, 31–33, 32f, 33t
   overview of, 135–36, 138–39, 142–44
   problematic versus nonproblematic, 2–3
   scope and prevalence, 26–31, 28t, 29f, 30f, 34–35
ideology, correctability and, 125–27, 125t
immigration and refugee misperceptions
   attitudinal effects of policy facts, 92–97, 93f, 95t, 96f
   identification of (*see* identification of misperceptions)
   inductive reasoning leading to, 69–70
   issue relevance and inductive reasoning, 65
   media coverage and, 36, 38, 39t, 42–45, 45f
   misleading rhetoric and, 42, 65, 69–70, 118
   partisanship and, 33, 33t, 81–92, 83t, 84f, 85f, 87t
   prevalence of, 29–31, 29f, 30f, 94–95, 95t, 122t, 122–23
   scope of, 26–31, 28t, 34–35
   See also policy approval and priorities, effect of policy-current information on

implied misinformation, 16
indifference to policy corrections, 119–21, 131, 134
inductive reasoning
  catalysts for, 58–60
  causal inference of policy facts, 86–87, 87t, 90–91
  concept of, 12–13, 56–57
  implications for agenda-setting, 72–74
  as information-seeking, 58–60
  issue relevance and, 60–66, 62f, 64t
  versus other types of cognition, 57–58, 64–65, 72–73
  policy misperceptions arising from, 11, 66–72, 67t, 133
inflation rate misperceptions, 17–18, 17f
informational utility model, 59–60
information environment. See media coverage, policy gap in; misinformation
Inglis, Rob, 40
innumeracy, 27
intentionality, attributions of, 67–69, 68t
interpretation of policy information
  attitudinal effects of policy facts, 92–97, 93f, 95t, 96f, 133–34
  beliefs and opinions compared to, 79–80
  difficulties of establishing causality about, 75–76, 97, 136
  information-processing theory and, 79–81
  partisan implications of policy facts, 81–92, 83t, 84f, 85f, 87t, 97, 133–34
  studies examining correction effects on, 77–79, 78t
interview approach
  eliciting misperceptions with, 23–26, 34–35, 142–43
  interview protocol, 20–23, 21t, 22t
  overview of, 19–20
  participant recruitment and demographics, 20–23, 21t, 22t
issue relevance, inductive reasoning and, 60–66, 62f, 64t
Ivanova, Ana, 38
Iyengar, Shanto, 69

Jerit, 55

Kahneman, D., 90

Klein, Ezra, 139–40
Knobloch, Silvia, 59
knowledge, curse of, 36–37, 49–50
Krosnick, Jon, 29
Krugman, Paul, 117–18
Kuklinski, James H., 99–100

late-night comedy, 143–44
learning
  learned beliefs, 57, 72–73
  personal relevance and, 60
  political satire as channel for, 143–44
  See also inductive reasoning
Lippmann, Walter, 10–11, 57, 116
Lodge, Milton, 86
Lovett, John, 38
Lucid, 61, 67, 82, 92–93, 100, 127
Lupia, Arthur, 2–3

McCaughey, Betsy, 14–15
McCombs, Maxwell E., 38
meaning avoidance, 80
media coverage
  "Americans don't care about policy" narrative, 120
  biases exacerbated by, 16
  consequences for public knowledge, 12–13, 54–55
  content analysis of, 42–45, 44t, 45f
  criticisms of and literature on, 37–38
  curse of knowledge, 36–37, 49–50
  national debt coverage case study, 50–54, 53t
  novelty bias in, 36–37, 47–49, 54, 120–21
  overview of, 36–37, 133
  social media, 55, 141–42
  strategy frames in, 36–37, 45–50, 52–54
  types of policy information in, 38–42, 39t
  See also policy-current information; policy-outcome information; policy-potential information
Medicaid, 40–41, 42, 48–49, 141, 142f
Medicare misperceptions
  identification of (see identification of misperceptions)
  media coverage and, 40, 42–45, 44t, 45f
  prevalence of, 25, 26–31, 28t, 29f, 34–35
mental models, dismantling of, 118

Mettler, Suzanne, 1–2, 11, 49
misinformation
  about Social Security, 61, 63–64
  dissemination of, 55
  implied, 16
  inductive reasoning versus, 74
  misleading rhetoric, 42, 65, 69–70, 118
  misperceptions arising from, 7–8, 10, 14–15, 17–18, 19, 56–57
  misperceptions versus, 135
  See also "fake news"
misleading rhetoric, 42, 65, 69–70, 118
Moore, Tim, 142f
MSNBC, coverage of national debt, 50–54, 53t
Mulvaney, Mick, 16

Nadeau, Richard, 59–60
national debt misperceptions
  contextual fact-checking of, 130–31, 130f
  correction of, 123–27, 124f, 125t
  identification of (see identification of misperceptions)
  inductive reasoning leading to, 11, 70–72
  media coverage and, 50–54, 53t
  partisanship and, 33, 33t, 81–92, 83t, 84f, 85f, 87t
  prevalence of, 29–31, 29f, 30f, 122t, 122–23
  scope of, 26–31, 28t, 34–35
  See also policy approval and priorities, effect of policy-current information on
News and Observer, 141–42
news coverage. See media coverage, policy gap in
New York Times
  coverage of national debt, 50–54, 53t
  policy gaps in coverage, 43–45, 45f
  Upshot column, 139–40
Niemi, Richard G., 59–60
novelty bias, 36–37, 47–49, 54, 120–21
Nyhan, Brendan, 14–15, 31, 75

Obama, Barack, misperceptions about birthplace/religion of, 135
  competence and, 3

origins of, 17–18, 19
partisan bias shaping, 7
prevalence of, 29–31, 30f
Ocasio-Cortez, Alexandria, 120–21
opinion disconnect, 80
opinions, effect of policy-current information on
  discussion of, 114–15
  implications of, 136–37
  information-processing theory and, 79–80
  misperceptions measured in, 101–2, 103t
  overview of, 98–99
  policy accuracy, 109–10, 109f
  policy approval, 102, 110–11, 110f
  policy opinions, 111–14, 111f, 112t, 113t
  policy priorities, 102–8, 112t
  study design, 100–1
  study goals, 99–100
  See also attitudes, political

Palin, Sarah, 7
partisanship and partisan identity
  attitudinal effects of policy facts, 92–97, 93f, 95t, 96f, 133–34
  beliefs shaped by, 4–6
  candidate-centered misperceptions and, 6–8
  misperceptions shaped by, 15–16
  partisan implications of policy facts, 81–92, 83t, 84f, 85f, 87t, 97, 133–34
  partisan surmise, 4, 5–6
  policy outcomes and, 5–6, 13
  prevalence of misconceptions and, 32f, 33, 33t
  resistance based in, 118–19
  See also bias
Pasek, Josh, 29
Patterson, Thomas E., 39–40
people holding misperceptions, characteristics of, 31–33, 32f, 33t
Pinker, Stephen, 50
Planned Parenthood, 122t, 123–27, 124f, 125t
pocketbook voting, 79

policy approval and priorities, effect of
  policy-current information on
    discussion of, 114–15
    implications of, 136–37
    information-processing theory
      and, 79–81
    misperceptions measured in, 101–2, 103t
    policy accuracy, 109–10, 109f
    policy approval, 102, 110–11, 110f
    policy opinions, 111–14
    policy priorities, 102–8, 112t
    study design, 100–1
    study goals, 99–100
policy-current information
  attitudinal effects of, 92–97, 93f, 95t, 96f
  content analysis of, 42–45, 44t, 45f
  definition of, 38–39, 41
  examples of, 39t
  importance of, 41–42
  integrating into media coverage, 139–42, 142f
  partisan implications of, 81–92, 83t, 84f, 85f, 87t
  public appetite for, 127–29, 128f, 129t, 131–32, 137–38
  studies examining corrective effects of, 77–79, 78t
  systematic barriers to, 45–50
  See also policy approval and priorities, effect of policy-current information on
policy-outcome information
  attitudinal effects of, 92–97, 93f, 95t, 96f
  content analysis of, 42–45, 44t, 45f
  definition of, 38–39, 40–41
  examples of, 39t
  partisan implications of, 5–6, 13, 81–92, 83t, 84f, 85f, 87t, 133–34
  studies examining correction effects of, 77–79, 78t
policy-potential information
  content analysis of, 42–45, 44t, 45f
  definition of, 38–40
  examples of, 39t
political attitudes. *See* attitudes, political
political interest, factual beliefs and, 32, 32f

political satire, 143–44
PolitiFact, 15, 61, 70
"post-truth," 4
preferences
  distortion of, 9–10
  in functioning democracy, 2
prevalence of policy misperceptions, 29–31, 30f, 45–50
priorities. *See* policy approval and priorities, effect of policy-current information on
Public Opinion (Lippmann), 57, 116
Pulitzer Prize Board, 139–40

rationalizing policy facts, 87, 87t
reasoning, inductive. *See* inductive reasoning
Refugee Act, 36
refugees. *See* immigration and refugee misperceptions
Reifler, Jason, 31
relevance, inductive reasoning and, 60–66, 62f, 64t
Republican partisanship. *See* partisanship and partisan identity
resistance to policy corrections, 117–19, 131, 134
retrospective voting, 5, 41, 79
rhetoric, misleading, 42, 65, 69–70, 118
Roberts, David, 141
Ryan, Paul, 54

Schafer, Mike S., 38
Schmidt, Andreas, 38
scope of misperceptions, measuring
  confidence measures, 29–30, 29f, 31
  distribution, 29–30, 29f
  kinds of people holding misperceptions, 31–33, 32f, 33t
  prevalence of policy misperceptions, 29–31, 30f
  question format, 27–29, 28t
  survey administration, 26–27
September 11 attack misconceptions, 7, 30–31, 30f
service journalism, 140
Shaw, Donald L., 38

SNAP. *See* food stamp policy misconceptions
social media, 55, 141–42
Social Security misperceptions
   attributions of intentionality in, 67–69, 68*t*
   biases contributing to, 16
   correction of, 123–27, 124*f*, 125*t*
   identification of (*see* identification of misperceptions)
   implied misinformation, 16
   issue relevance and inductive reasoning, 60–66, 62*f*, 64*t*
   media coverage and, 55
   partisanship and, 81–92, 83*t*, 84*f*, 85*f*, 87*t*
   prevalence of, 29–31, 29*f*
   See also policy approval and priorities, effect of policy-current information on
social utility of information, 66
social welfare program misperceptions
   identification of (*see* identification of misperceptions)
   partisanship and, 33, 33*t*
   prevalence of, 29–31, 29*f*, 30*f*
   survey questions, 28*t*
   See also food stamp policy misconceptions; Medicaid; TANF policy misconceptions
sociotropic voting, 79
Sood, Gaurav, 29
Soroka, Stuart N., 48
spending misperceptions
   correction of, 123–27, 124*f*, 125*t*
   identification of (*see* identification of misperceptions)
   partisanship and, 33, 33*t*
   prevalence of, 29–31, 29*f*, 30*f*, 122*t*, 122–23
   survey question wording, 28*t*
static-policy corrections, effectiveness of, 121–23, 122*t*
strategy frames, 36–37, 46–47, 52–54
Sullivan, Margaret, 37–38
Susterern, Greta Van, 53

systematic barriers to policy-current coverage
   curse of knowledge, 36–37, 49–50
   novelty bias, 36–37, 47–49, 54
   strategy frames, 36–37, 46–47, 52–54

Taber, Charles S., 86
TANF policy misconceptions
   correction of, 123–27, 124*f*, 125*t*
   identification of (*see* identification of misperceptions)
   partisanship and, 81–92, 83*t*, 84*f*, 85*f*, 87*t*
   prevalence of, 29–31, 30*f*, 122*t*, 122–23
   See also entitlement program misperceptions; policy approval and priorities, effect of policy-current information on; social welfare program misperceptions
tax misperceptions
   correction of, 123–27, 124*f*, 125*t*
   identification of (*see* identification of misperceptions)
   partisanship and, 33, 33*t*, 81–92, 83*t*, 84*f*, 85*f*, 87*t*
   prevalence of, 29–31, 29*f*, 30*f*, 122*t*, 122–23
taxonomic similarity, misperceptions arising from, 70–72
Tea Party movement, 53–54
Trump, Donald
   immigration rhetoric of, 42, 65, 70, 118, 120–21
   inauguration crowd size, 17–18
   media coverage of, 39–40, 54–55
   misinformation about, 7
   misinformation used by, 8–9

Upshot column, *New York Times*, 139–40
USA Today
   coverage of national debt, 50–54, 53*t*
   policy gap in coverage by, 43–45, 45*f*

vaccine misperceptions, 17–18, 17*f*, 34
Vander Wielen, Ryan J., 4

Vox.com, 139–40

Walsh, John, 53
Washington Post, coverage of national debt, 50–54, 53t
will to believe, 11–12
Wlezien, Christopher, 48

women, political knowledge of, 32–33, 63

Yglesias, Matt, 139–40

Zaller, John, 64–65, 74
Zillmann, Dolf, 59